Colin Pressdee's
Welsh Coastal Cookery

BBC BOOKS

This book is published to accompany a BBC Radio Wales series which was first
broadcast in 1995 and was produced by Prospect Cymru Wales Ltd
Executive Producer Rhys John
Producer Mark John

Published by BBC Books,
an imprint of BBC Worldwide Publishing,
BBC Worldwide Limited, Woodlands,
80 Wood Lane, London W12 0TT

First published 1995

ISBN 0 563 37136 6

Design and illustrations by Louise Morley
Map by Venture Graphics
Cover photographs *Stuffed Shoulder of Autumn Lamb with Wild Mushrooms* (see page 98), *Sea Bass
with Buerre Blanc* (see page 72) and *Snowdon Pudding with Strawberry and Gin Sauce* (see page 152)
by David Ward and sponsored by Welsh Food Promotions
Food photographs by Ian Bodenham

Set in Palatino and Bellevue
Printed and bound in Great Britain by Clays Ltd, St Ives plc
Colour origination by Scanagraphics, Cardiff
Colour printing by Lawrence Allen Ltd, Weston-super-Mare
Cover printed by Clays Ltd, St Ives plc

About the Author

Colin Pressdee was born in Swansea and grew up in and around the Gower peninsular. He has a passion for food and fishing and his career running a seafood export company and several restaurants in Swansea and Mumbles bear witness to this. Winner of the Glenfiddich Award for Regional Writer of the Year for his food and wine articles in *Wales on Sunday* during 1989, Colin writes regular articles and restaurant reviews for a variety of publications. His first book, *Streetwise Cookery* (published in 1992), accompanied the BBC Radio Wales *Streetlife* programmes which he presented, and he writes regular recipe and fact sheets for the *Ray Gravel's Morning Programme* listeners. Colin has made many television programmes, notably as presenter of the cookery and food section of *See You Sunday* for BBC Wales and *Summer Scene*, broadcast live from the Garden Festival at Ebbw Vale in 1992. He has also appeared with Wynford Vaughan-Thomas in *The Coastline of Wales*, and with Keith Floyd and Gary Rhodes, expounding the culinary delights of Welsh fare. He continued to celebrate these delights in his thirteen-part BBC Radio Wales series, recorded on location around the coastline of Wales and broadcast in 1995. Colin currently runs a consultancy business and spends his time equally between London and Wales.

About Welsh Food Promotions

Wales is well known for its spectacular inland and coastal scenery, but its cuisine is not as well known. Welsh Food Promotions through its brand 'Taste of Wales' is continually placing Welsh food in the culinary spotlight, as its remit is to develop and market the Welsh food industry from the farm gate to the dinner plate. With the help of some of Wales' top cookery personalities, such as Colin Pressdee, our aim is being achieved.

Welsh cattle and sheep are reared on lush pasturelands giving the beef and lamb its sweet taste, while the 750 miles of coastline are home to a vast array of fish and shellfish. Add to these some of the purest mineral and spring waters in the world, 60 varieties of delicious farmhouse cheeses, and fresh vegetables, and it's easy to see why more and more people are searching for their own taste of Wales.

For a copy of the *Taste of Wales Gazetteer*, listing more than 300 places to eat and stay, or the *Food Producers' Directory*, or for any information on Welsh food please contact Welsh Food Promotions on (01222) 640456.

ACKNOWLEDGMENTS

Thanks to producer Mark John and researcher Sarah Tavner for their enthusiasm and company, to the many friends, old and new, we encountered on our travels around the coastline of Wales, and to all those who contributed their thoughts and recipes.

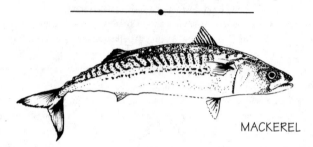

MACKEREL

CONTENTS

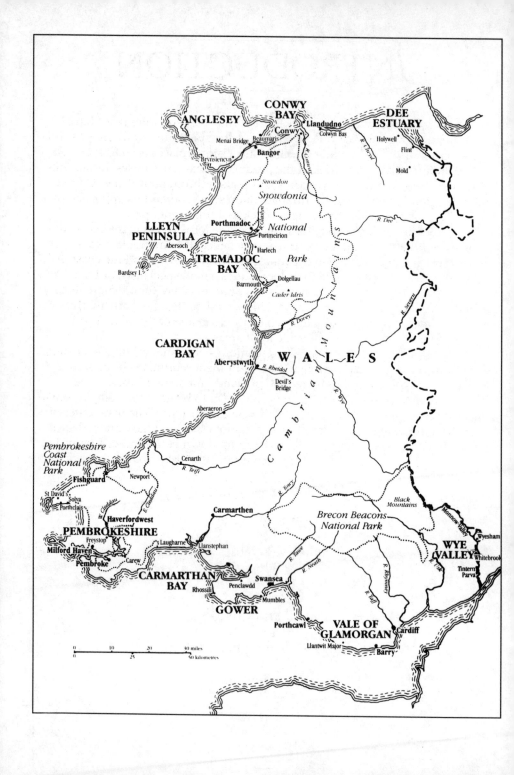

INTRODUCTION

This collection of recipes is taken from the vast repertoire that I have accumulated over the last three decades. I have spent numerous days fishing the coast and rivers, walking the cliffs and visiting places around the coast. Most importantly, I have cooked the produce in my own houses, restaurants and wine bars, and at friends' farms and houses throughout Wales. On radio and television I have aimed to stimulate interest in food and its appreciation at every level from a light snack to a full dinner party.

The recipes are my own style for using the fine local Welsh ingredients, and some are from the numerous enthusiastic chefs and home cooks I have met over the years and whom we encounter on our travels around the coast. All the ingredients are available from local shops, small specialists, or the main supermarkets. Where more obscure local variations were found, more readily available produce can be substituted. This would be the case particularly with such items as salt marsh lamb, which rarely gains recognition outside specific local areas.

All the recipes use standard cooking techniques of frying, grilling, poaching, roasting, baking and casseroling. The equipment required is basic; a food processor or liquidizer will be handy for some recipes.

The recipes are set out in sections to enable them to be used for a single-course meal, or combined to form a more elaborate dinner party. The main criterion for the latter is that the styles of dishes do not clash, and flavours in dishes chosen build up as the courses proceed, toning down at the end of a feast. The same applies to wines chosen to accompany the dinner party or snack.

AROUND THE WELSH COASTLINE

The journey around the coastline of Wales begins in the lower Wye Valley, down to the Bristol Channel, where a fast ebbing tide takes us west past the Vale of Glamorgan, the Gower peninsula, Carmarthen Bay, and eventually to the most remote islands off the coast of Pembrokeshire.

From here we travel north into the sweep of Cardigan Bay, eventually reaching the morning shadows of the mighty Cambrian mountains of Cader Idris and Snowdonia. The Lleyn peninsula reaches west to Bardsey Island, then back east, passing the Isle of Anglesey and the Vale of Clwyd, into the Dee estuary where our journey ends.

In this relatively short voyage, we pass some of the most magnificent scenery and coastal land forms imaginable. Millions of people have gazed in awe at the great headland of Worms Head at Rhossili, and the towering Stack Rocks of Pembroke, as the Atlantic breakers pound into them, sending spray hundreds of feet into the air. Yet a few miles away from both are found tranquil, sheltered estuaries where cattle and sheep graze and sea birds bob on placid waters.

Some of the most majestic stretches of beach are found in the south. In the north, mountains rise steeply from the rocky shores. Numerous rivers channel their way from the well drenched mountains into the bays, making estuaries that are a haven for sea and land creatures and farm animals alike.

The tides bring a diversity to both rocky headlands and river mouths. The Bristol Channel, noted for one of the greatest tides in the world, will reveal in some areas vast expanses of sands and mud flats, and in others, hundreds of acres of rocky terrain on the inter-tidal zones. These tides affect many estuaries miles up the river valleys into the centres of farmland regions.

On the Welsh coastline we find rocky headlands, sandy beaches, storm pebble banks, sand dunes, steep cliffs, planar bays, flooded valleys, deep water rias, craggy islands, salt marshes and lush lowlands. Each area of coast and the sea beyond has been farmed or fished for time immemorial. The sea and land have been providers of the most diverse range of natural and farmed foods.

In one tiny area alone we can find a whole array of shellfish, from humble cockles and winkles to the highly prized lobster and crawfish. Yards away is an estuary brimming with everything from whitebait and prawns to salmon, sewin and eels. The creeks can be full of wild ducks, samphire and seabeet, sharing space with spring lambs grazing on the salt marshes. Close by, a small fishing port lands sea bass, turbot, sole, plaice and mackerel amongst its diverse catch.

Some southern areas escape winter frosts and provide agricultural produce – root vegetables, leeks, cabbages and cauliflowers – every month of the year, and are the first in Britain to pull early new potatoes when other areas have yet to smell the spring. Rich, lush valleys have been renowned for milk and beef production, and the steepest mountains are no threat to Welsh lambs in search of natural hill pastures.

The topography of Wales and its coastline breaks areas into small patches. Most farms are tiny, and numerous small villages and towns straddle the river mouths. Many areas were virtually self-sufficient until the last few centuries, and hence provided everything from the daily milk and bread to bacon, lamb and beef, and vegetables from the land. The sea gave fish and shellfish to vary the diets of the locals.

With industrialization and commercialization of areas, large fishing fleets searching for hake and cod grew up in Milford Haven, Swansea and Cardiff in the south, and smaller ones in Conwy and Bangor in the north. As these fleets have gradually died out, a whole plethora of small fleets has emerged, fishing a vast range of every species. Bass, lobsters, salmon, sewin, sole and skate are now the important cash catches.

Farming has undergone changes recently, with milk quotas on one hand and an insatiable demand for lamb on the other. Yet in a world of rapid change it is still quite amazing what a range of produce can be found around the Welsh coastline and hinterland. Some are exploited beyond any commercial sense, while other stocks disappear from ravages of other foreign predators. Some areas are being managed to ensure supplies for the future, while others are being polluted out of existence.

In each area there is still a great array of food products. Testimony to the quality and diversity of the produce is the number of restaurants and hotels that have sprung up in the past decade, many preening themselves for their use of local ingredients. There are many small cafés, bars and large hotels that have striven to become known for their fare, whether on a purely local or even international basis. On our trip we aimed to seek out as many of these as possible, and chat to the cooks, chefs, suppliers and customers to see how they make use of the food from the Welsh coastline.

We begin our tour in the Wye Valley at Tintern, renowned as far back as 1188 when Geraldis Cambrensis wrote of the great winter salmon of the River Wye. The monks of Tintern Abbey planted vines here, and in recent decades new vineyards have developed, taking advantage of the sunny south-facing slopes of the lower valley. Wordsworth's sylvan Wye has some fine old mature woodlands that abound in wild mushrooms through the warmer months, and on the edges numerous small farms rear pigs, ducks and geese, all fit for the best tables.

We were fortunate to catch a salmon at Wyesham in the 'Rabbits' Hole' pool. A mere six-pounder, it was returned to the river to continue its life and hopefully procreate. The Crown Inn, just above the tidal reaches at Bigsweir Bridge, helped us sample the delights of this area.

The Vale of Glamorgan skirts the once beautiful valleys that were ravaged by coal mining and steel-making. The coastal waters are muddy from the silt carried by the great River Severn, but fish do exist here, as all Wye salmon travel up-channel through this water.

Many of the rivers have been cleaned after the industrial demise and now salmon run on the rivers Taff, Ely, Ogmore, Neath and Tawe, where two decades ago such a scene would have seemed impossible.

The industrialization led to development of seaside resorts where the workers could relax and enjoy themselves. There, the cheapest fodder was fish and chips, but with good quality fish and freshly cooked chips, these are now almost a delicacy in many restaurants.

The Gower peninsula is where I was brought up. As a child I was fascinated by lobsters, oysters, sea bass and almost anything you could find and eat from the sea. I soon became interested in cooking the produce myself, and what could be a finer meal than fish and shellfish I had caught that day?

I can remember the very cranny where I caught my first crab and lobster; the very rock where I perched and cast for my first bass at Whiteshell; the smell of the fresh foods cooking, and the appetite that a day on the seashore gave me. I would scrabble over the rocks for crab and lobster while my father sometimes went out in the boat for bass and mackerel. Someone else would shove a push net across the beach for prawns. We would pick mussels and winkles from the rocks, gather the seaweed laverbread, or search the cliffs for wild mushrooms.

The local farmers exchanged Gower new potatoes and cauliflowers for a few mackerel. At night we might take out the drag net and trawl deep in the dark water for sole, plaice, skate and even squid and cuttlefish. I can remember returning dozens of spider crabs from the lobster pots, not to mention kilos of whelks, conger eels, whiting, mullet, pollock and fiddler crabs, which today are all prized.

There is no finer smell than that of fresh food cooking as one wades salty from the sea. At Rhossili we had a fishing hut aptly named Kitchen Corner, the last point before the causeway to Worms Head. Here we caught and cooked everything. We would have hut feasts of the catch, cooked on a small primus stove and a feeble two-burner Calor Gas hob. But what was turned out with such limited facilities was finer than most restaurants would even aspire to.

Mumbles, the west part of Swansea Bay, was one of the largest oyster fisheries in Europe, exporting millions of the delicacy every year to be the food of the poor in the cities. Over-fishing and pollution had finished the industry by the thirties, but now there are healthy signs of stocks regenerating in the bay.

North Gower is synonymous with cockles, mussels and laverbread. The villages of Crofty and Penclawdd house the producers who rake or collect their supply, cook, then sell in Swansea and other markets as totally integrated family businesses. Many also grow vegetables or farm sheep on the salt marshes, or even trawl for fish for extra income.

Swansea itself has a considerable fishing fleet of small boats, which has replaced the old, traditional, deep-water fishery. A visit to the fish docks shows a variety of the freshest possible produce from the short one-day voyages. The retail market is where many of these fish appear on slabs, alongside other local produce of Gower: vegetables, shellfish, bakery and dairy products, and the finest local Welsh lamb and beef.

Carmarthen Bay sweeps from Gower to Tenby and is the delta for many rivers, including the Loughor, Towy and Taf. The rich fishing grounds were probably not as noted as the ten miles of sand where the hell-raising, dare-devil car races were contested in the 1930s. It is a truly agricultural area, with only one main market town, Carmarthen. No wonder it inspired Dylan Thomas to write *Under Milk Wood* to epitomize the gentle, yet earthy, way of life. Rich, fertile farmland and productive seas and estuaries give a range of foods that motivate many home cooks and part-time restaurateurs. Our first stop found Ena Thomas in Carmarthen market, where she can produce wonders for any household on whatever budget. The Rees brothers provide Carmarthen ham, salmon, sewin, and all fish and shellfish, plus finest Welsh lamb, beef and dairy produce.

The legendary large man of the restaurant business – twenty stone of solid Welsh muscle – Bill Hill, late of the Salutation, Nantgaredig (valley of the gentle stream), now resides on the very 'heron-priested estuary' where Dylan wrote, upstream in his boathouse at Laugharne. Hen Dafan (the old pub) is now Bill and Judith's place, serving anything Bill can catch from his boat, rake from the shore, shoot with his twelve-bore, pick from the hedges or grow in the garden. He augments his supplies from anyone else local, and believes everyone has his appetite. Whatever may be lacking in finesse is compensated for in ambience and generosity.

The English built a row of castles across Pembroke to defend the southern area. The 'Landsker' is on the same line as the January 32ºF isotherm, below which milder winters make winter crops abundant. All types of vegetables escape the frost, and early new potatoes were a great bonanza before imports began arriving from the more distant farms of the Mediterranean and even of the southern hemisphere.

Pembroke turkey has become as famous as Aylesbury duck. Great shoots are organized on the estates. Lobster and crab fishing reaps its harvest from the rocky coastline. The oyster industry, second to Mumbles in the nineteenth century, has re-established at Carew. Little England, as it's known, is hardly short of produce or eager customers from locals, industrialists and tourists.

Chef/hotelier Taffy Wooles has been in the kitchen for over thirty years and still cooks every day. He has roast more turkeys than anyone I know, but still considers it very fine meat and now such wonderful value.

North Pembrokeshire is more rugged and beautiful, the Coast National Park being a designated area for preservation. The islands of Skomer, Skokholm and Ramsey have great colonies of sea birds that feast on the bounty of the oceans. This is the home of the perky little puffin and the magnificent gannet colony.

Tiny fishing ports, formerly stone-exporting quarries, give shelter to fleets of small working and pleasure boats. The Welsh names of the villages and headlands – Porthgain, Abereiddy, Penclegyr, Tresinwen – evoke the more homely style of living and hospitality. Several little pubs and restaurants can produce dazzlingly fresh seafoods and farm produce, yet all depend on the elements, tides and mood of the locals.

Fishguard harbour is the ferry port for Ireland and offers some of the warm Celtic hospitality on a large scale, the hotels and restaurants having a more commercial, enthusiastic feel. But the coast from here to St David's and around the sweep of St Bride's Bay must house the best secrets of the entire coastline.

Although butterfly farms and aquariums show the commercial side of the tourist industry, you can still find numerous fishing families who will dress fresh crabs, spin for a dozen or so mackerel, catch a bucket of prawns or even pick a sack of laverbread. Jemima's near Haverfordwest, the Harbour Lights at the old granite quarry port of Porthgain, and Tates in Fishguard are all fine examples of these opportunist eateries.

The coast from Fishguard to Aberystwyth, although it has fewer spectacular landforms, is more gentle, with high cliffs and large bays interspersed with tiny coves and river mouths. The Teifi Valley dominates the area, with numerous dairy and mixed farms. The river itself has probably the most exciting salmon and sewin fishing to be found. Geraldis commented on the spectacular sight of fish leaping the great falls at Cenarth. Gareth Edwards said to catch a salmon here made the heart beat faster than scoring a try for Wales!

Flour mills and cheese farms are the food finds in this area. Restaurant names have reflected this over the years. The Mill, Nest, Pantry, Hive, Felingwm (valley with a mill), Plough, all suggest good homely farm-style cooking.

The harbour at Aberaeron (the mouth of the river Aeron) brings together the produce from the land and sea at the Hive, where people sit and watch the fishing-boat-bobbing sea and eat crab, sewin, home-baked cakes and honey.

The Teifi Valley is large and mature for the present size of the river. The upper reaches of the Teifi, which used to drain the Cambrian mountains, were captured by the Ystwyth and, in turn, by the Rheidol at the precipitous waterfalls at Devil's Bridge. The rejuvenated river almost forms the boundary where the terrain becomes the familiar, rugged, mountainous heights of North Wales. Here, the coastal vales are narrow, the mountains rising the three thousand feet at Cader Idris (the great chair) just a few miles inland.

Heavy rainfall drains to the turbulent rivers Dovey and Mawddach, where salmon, sewin and trout abound. The large estuaries are home for wildlife and farm grazing. The fishing port, Barmouth, has the most industrious fleet in the area, scooping scallops, queens, lobsters, crabs and prime flatfish by the ton.

Dolgellau is the old centre of the farming trade in Welsh mountain lamb. Slate quarries brought more wealth, and many great houses were built from the local stone and are now the havens of hospitality tourism. Their names are big and grand: Penmaenuchaf, Dolmelynllyn, and their menus specialize in fish from the bay and lamb from the hills just a few miles apart.

Snowdonia is the most impressive yet diverse of all areas. Miles of waste from defunct slate quarries and a disused nuclear power station are just a few miles from the Glaslyn estuary, which has the most perfect postcard aspect of all, looking north to Snowdon itself. This inspired Portmeirion, one of the most eccentric developments in the world, created by Victorian architect Clough Williams-Ellis. The ornate, miniature, Italianesque village has inspired artists and television producers alike. The tranquillity of the village and estuary is a perfect setting for the Hotel Portmeirion which aspires to fine gastronomy while coping with the inevitable torrent of tourists.

Tremadog Bay is renowned for its fine seafoods, the quay at Porthmagog landing monkfish, turbot, sole and brill. The enclosed marsh behind the Victorian breakwater is a haven for wild ducks and geese, and the smaller snipe and woodcock.

The mighty castle at Harlech, which has probably the most commanding position of any Welsh edifice, has more recently been synonymous with traditional Welsh hospitality, just as was given to the bards in olden times. In the mountains behind, the mansion Maes y Neuadd serves fine fare and has developed its own business producing herbs, preserves and chutneys.

The Lleyn peninsula ends with Bardsey Island, where the monks used to take sheep by boat to roam and feed on the lush, sea-sprayed, guano-fertilized pastures. The flavour of a 'weather' – a lamb that had spent a full winter grazing there – was renowned to be the finest, richest mutton of all. The monks always had good taste.

At the tiny resort of Abersoch is one of the longest-standing restaurants listed by the *Good Food Guide*. Porth Tocyn Hotel has been a haven for fine food for generations, and still offers the most homely Welsh atmosphere with local produce. The lone Michelin Star in Wales has been earned by Plas Bedogroes, where Chris Chown, whose family all have local connections, cooks in sumptuous style.

On the north site, in an old granite-quarrying village, is the Welsh Language Centre Nant Gwytheyrn in a spectacular location with pebbly storm beaches battered by Atlantic seas. The vast area is full of wildlife, hedgerow plants, berries and fungi. Many locals shoot and gather fodder here, finding eager markets in the famous hotels.

The Isle of Anglesey is separated from the mainland by a narrow but very turbulent channel. It was well fortified at either end with the great castles of Caernarfon and Beaumaris. These brought great wealth and standing to the area, and the main ferryport at Hollyhead brings a constant flow of traffic and business. The land is low, gentle and fertile, producing some of the finest beef to be found in Britain, and a Smithfield supreme champion a few years ago.

The Sea Zoo at Brynsiencyn is a fine example of large-scale catering for the public, relying almost entirely on organic and free-range produce and home-caught fish. In Beaumaris the feel is rich and relaxed, epitomized by the warmth of welcome and stylish food at the Old Bull's Head, which has been the hostelry of note for decades.

The churning waters of the Menai are rich for bass fishing, oysters and mussels. One of the largest highly organized shellfisheries is found at Bangor, where the Myti mussel plant sends daily hundreds of tons of purified, cleaned, packaged mussels to markets all over Britain and Europe. The proprietors, Kim and Val Mold, also sell their produce in their own restaurant.

The smallest house in the world is on the quay at Conwy and its kitchen is somewhat cramped. A few yards away several fishing boats daily land their trawlings from Conwy Bay. The seas here are well sheltered by Anglesey from the Atlantic storms and, hence, regular landings are made.

The river is famous for its salmon, and many fine restaurants thrive in the sheltered valley, serving the best pickings from the river, sea and land. The religious connection is prevalent again, as one of the best in the area is the Old Rectory at Glan Conwy, testimony to the frugal lifestyle of the clergy in the past.

The great seafront of the Victorian resort of Llandudno has numerous magnificent old hotels, many of which are family-run. A particular discovery is the Merrion Hotel for a true family feel with the best value dinner in Wales. More lavish is the St Tudno, which has been a civilized retreat since the Blands took it over in the early 1970s.

The final part of the trek takes us through the Vale of Clwyd. Fifty miles away is one of the wettest areas of Britain. The coastal resort of Rhyl is one of the driest, with record sunshine as it basks in the rain shadow of Snowdonia. The coastline is plain and quite uninteresting. There are no featured landforms to speak of. The rolling landscape is far removed from the Cambrian mountains. The River Dee is slow and gentle, meandering its way lazily through Llangollen to the sea near Chester. But the area has the overflow wealth from the Midlands and Merseyside. It is a place of comfort where the bishops set up their finest palace in 1714, at Northrop, just inside the Welsh border in 150 acres of parkland, now a hotel, Soughton Hall. Having followed much of the path of Geraldis, passing so many rugged yet stunning areas, it seems fitting to be entertained in a manner fit for a bishop at this hall. The great estates used to hunt for their supper, but now close by is a venison farm which will provide the meat for our sumptuous concluding meal.

———————————•———————————

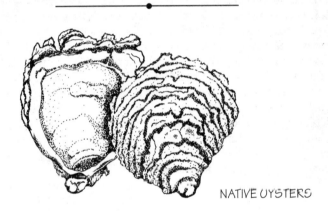

NATIVE OYSTERS

STARTERS - FISH

MUSSELS

These are found all around the coast of Wales, particularly at the low ebb of a spring tide. They are best where the water is clean and rich in plankton. The finest mussels are those harvested while still small and free from encrustations of barnacles, and the meat is sweet and succulent. The largest producers are in Conwy and the Menai Straits, although many other fishermen gather them by hand from west Wales, Carmarthen Bay and Gower.

You can collect your own mussels from many beaches, estuaries and headlands at low tide, but always check that it is a pollution-free area. Try to find clean mussels about 5 cm (2 in) long, and pick them as far down the tide mark as possible.

You can buy live mussels in fishmongers and supermarkets. Although they are sold every month, I find them best in the colder wintertime when there's an 'R' in the month – September to April always was the traditional oyster and mussel season.

Always check mussels carefully. Discard any that are open and will not close naturally if tapped. Some may be full of mud yet tightly closed, so I always pound them thoroughly in a bowl of fresh water, then individually examine them while removing the beard or 'bissus' by which the mussel attaches itself to the rocks. This is not poisonous but would be indigestible eaten in quantity. Always cook mussels in a covered pan for 3 minutes so the steam will destroy any remaining bacteria. If any mussels remain closed after cooking, discard them.

Swansea market usually has boiled mussels on sale alongside the cockles. Provided these are fresh, they are useful for some dishes where cooked meats are required. They do not freeze well, however, as they acquire a powdery texture and fishy flavour after very little time. If you freeze your own mussels after cooking, cover them with the cold cooking liquor and they retain quality for several months.

COLD MUSSELS WITH GARLIC AND CORIANDER

The recipe for *Moules à la Marinière* has been written numerous times. If you want the basic *marinière*, follow this recipe until the mussels are steamed. For a more exotic version, you can serve this dish hot, but I find it very good on a cold platter.

Serves 4
1 tablespoon oil
225 g (8 oz) shallots, finely chopped
6 garlic cloves, finely chopped
300 ml (10 fl oz) dry white wine
6 bay leaves
1 sprig of fresh thyme
1.5 kg (3 lb) fresh mussels in the shell, scrubbed and bearded
salt and freshly ground black pepper
50 g (2 oz) bunch of fresh coriander, stalks removed
1 tablespoon sesame oil

*H*eat the oil and fry half the shallots and garlic for about 1 minute until just softening. Add the wine, bay leaves and thyme and cook for 3-5 minutes to develop the flavours. Add the mussels to the pan, cover tightly and cook for 3-5 minutes, shaking the pan frequently until the mussels are all open; discard any that remain closed. Remove from the heat and leave covered as they cool. This will retain all the moisture and succulence.

Pull away one shell from each of the mussels and arrange them in the remaining half-shell on a serving platter.

Check the cooking juices for salt, then boil until reduced to about 300 ml (10 fl oz). Leave to cool.

Place the remaining garlic, shallots and coriander stalks in a food processor. Strain the mussel juice to remove the bay, thyme and any grit, then add the juice to the processor with the sesame oil and a very generous twist of black pepper. Process to form a smooth sauce. Spoon over the mussels and top with fresh coriander leaves. Keep cool until served.

OYSTERS

Oysters were once plentiful around Wales, particularly in Swansea Bay, where the Romans established a fishery at Mumbles, and the waters of Milford Haven. However, over-fishing and pollution have depleted the stocks of the 'native' oyster.
Farmed rock oysters, indigenous to the Pacific, have now replenished some of the beds, and large fisheries are found at Carew and Conwy. Native oysters are making a slow revival in Swansea Bay and the straits opposite Benton Castle in the Haven. It would be good to see 'Benton Natives' revived on our menus! Many people acquire the taste for oysters if sampled in a cooked dish first. The irony, calcarious sea flavour is almost addictive once tasted, and the nuances combine very well in many dishes.

GRATIN OF OYSTERS WITH HERB CRUST

The toasted flavour of crisp garlic and sesame oil is quite exquisite and a surprising combination with oysters.

Serves 4
1 tablespoon oil
4 garlic cloves, crushed and chopped
100 g (4 oz) brown bread, slightly stale
4-5 large sprigs of fresh coriander
2-3 greens from spring onions
1 tablespoon sesame oil
100 g (4 oz) laverbread
16-24 oysters, shucked, retaining all juices and deep shells
½ teaspoon tabasco sauce
225 g (8 oz) coarse sea salt
2 lemons, cut into wedges

Pre-heat the oven to 230ºC/450ºF/gas 8. Heat the oil and fry the garlic until very golden and quite crisp. Remove from the pan to cool. Make a herb crust by processing the pieces of bread in a food processor. Add the crisp garlic. Reserve a few coriander leaves for garnish, chop the remainder and add to the processor with the spring onion greens. Mix until all ingredients are finely chopped. Add the garlicky oil and sesame oil and mix for a few seconds to form a herb crumble.

Mix the laverbread with some of the oyster juice and tabasco sauce to make a thick, flowing relish. Put a teaspoon into each deep shell and top with an oyster. Sprinkle the herby mix on to each.

Tip the salt into a large roasting tray and embed the oysters to stop them tilting during cooking. Place in the pre-heated oven for 3-4 minutes maximum to crispen the crust and just heat the oysters through, taking care not to overcook and shrivel them. Garnish generously with roughly chopped coriander leaves and lemon wedges.

_L_AVERBREAD

The other Swansea speciality is laverbread or bara lawr, the seaweed 'laver' (*porphyra umbilicalis*) which grows on the intertidal zone. Its dark, smooth appearance makes it distinctive. Traditionally, it is boiled for hours to render it to a thick purée, sold in the markets of south Wales. If gathered fresh, it can be deep-fried into tasty crisps. It can also be purchased in 200g (8oz) cans.

_D_EEP-FRIED COCKLES, MUSSELS AND LAVER WITH SPICY MAYONNAISE

If you cannot obtain freshly picked laver seaweed, use the outer leaves of spring cabbage, finely shredded. Self-raising flour gives a good crispness to the shellfish and seaweed when fried, but they must be partially dry so the amount of flour that coats them is not excessive.

Serves 4
450 g (1 lb) cockles and mussels, freshly cooked and shelled
100 g (4 oz) freshly picked laver seaweed or the outer leaves of spring cabbage
225 g (8 oz) self-raising flour
1 teaspoon paprika
1 litre (1¾ pints) sunflower or groundnut oil
sea salt and freshly ground black pepper
1 lemon, cut into wedges
3 tablespoons mayonnaise
2 teaspoons chilli sauce

Drain off any excess juice from the cockles and mussels but do not press or squeeze them. Wash the seaweed and cut into 5 cm (2 in) pieces. Squeeze dry in kitchen paper. If using cabbage, wash and shred it and shake off any excess water.

Mix together the flour and paprika and dust the mussels and cockles with the mixture, using a sieve to shake off the excess. Heat the oil and deep-fry the seafood for about 1 minute or until turning crisp and slightly golden. Drain and reserve. Repeat for the laver or cabbage, stirring this during cooking to keep the pieces separate. Season everything with salt and pepper and arrange on a warmed serving plate. Garnish with lemon wedges.

Mix together the mayonnaise and chilli sauce and serve with the seafoods.

———————•———————

COCKLES

Cockles are one of the specialities of Swansea market. Traditionally, they formed part of a breakfast with Welsh bacon and eggs. They are on sale daily from local suppliers.

The cockle is a small clam and hence can be adapted to a very wide range of cooking styles, from Mediterranean to American. Every year, Swansea market holds a Cockle Festival at the end of September, and local chefs demonstrate a wide range of dishes using fresh Penclawdd cockles.

Cockles are gathered from estuaries at low tide by raking the sand, then washing clean. In Gower they have been harvested since Roman times, and the fishery is still thriving at Penclawdd, fishing the sands of the Bury estuary. Like mussels, they are filter feeders and have to be cleansed and cooked thoroughly – a job best left to the cockle producers!

———————•———————

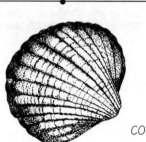

COCKLE

SMOKED MACKEREL WITH CARROT
AND CORIANDER SALAD

Mackerel frequents the Welsh coastline during the summer and autumn. Eaten fresh, its very oily flesh has the most silky flavour and texture. This makes it perfect for smoking, the oil keeping the flesh moist. Although now commonplace, it can still be part of a great menu. The freshest mackerel, simply cooked, is utterly delicious, and the natural oils it contains are very fine for one's health and natural body balance.

Serves 4
grated zest and juice of 1 lemon
2 tablespoons sesame oil
3 spring onions, white parts only, chopped
25 g (1 oz) bunch of fresh coriander, chopped
salt and freshly ground black pepper
450 g (1 lb) fresh young carrots
1 tablespoon sunflower oil
8 x 5 cm (2 in) rounds of bread for croûtons
1 garlic clove, crushed
4 x 100 g (4 oz) smoked mackerel fillets
½ teaspoon cayenne

Combine the lemon zest and juice, sesame oil, chopped spring onions, half the coriander and the salt and pepper. Thinly slice the carrots with a potato peeler or shred with a coarse grater. Add to the sesame mix and leave for 1 hour, stirring occasionally.

Heat the sunflower oil and fry the rounds of bread with the garlic and a dash of sesame oil until golden brown. Reserve.

Remove the skin and any fins and bones from the mackerel, cutting each fillet into three pieces.

Arrange the croûtons and carrot salad on plates, top with the smoked mackerel, sesame sauce and remaining coriander leaves, then sprinkle with the cayenne.

SQUID, CUTTLEFISH AND OCTOPUS

These strange creatures, best known in Mediterranean cuisine, have become popular in recent years as Brits become more adventurous on summer holidays. They are known as cephalopods, and all have a similar flavour and strange white, solid flesh. They are all cunning hunters with selective diets of other fish and shellfish.

Cuttlefish is the least popular, although the flesh is white and succulent. It was much favoured by the Romans, and is now popular in Spain. It has the highest yield of solid white body meat, and the distinctive solid white backbone. Conversely, the boneless octopus has large, powerful, tasty tentacles. Squid has the most succulent flesh of all.

Trawlers all around the Welsh coast frequently land big quantities of cuttlefish and squid, and these can be inexpensive in the summer months. Octopus, however, prefer warmer water and are rarely found in quantity in Wales – sensible creatures.

All these freeze quite well, but tend to discolour to purple as the strange pigments in the skin break down.

They are quite easy to prepare, as you can soak them without harming the solid flesh. The tentacles can be pulled away from the body with ease, and the tiny, silver ink sac from inside can be reserved. Between the tentacles you will find the 'beak' which literally pops out when squeezed, then the bunch of eight can be cut off in one. These should be washed vigorously to remove the tiny suckers, then sliced to the desired size. The solid backbone of the cuttlefish and the soft 'pen' of the squid are easily pulled from the body sac. The skin pulls away easily, leaving the solid body to cook whole or in pieces.

Many supermarkets sell squid ready prepared, but don't be put off a bargain if you have to do the work yourself.

———————•———————

CUTTLEFISH OR SQUID WITH CHARRED VEGETABLES

This uses the least expensive species, but is very quick to prepare and certainly delicious. The aim is to keep the textures of the fish and vegetables the same.

A grillomat is one of the most useful things for any kitchen, and has been my standard wedding present for years! Made by the French company Le Creuset, and others, it is simply a slab of cast iron with undulations to give the brown barbecue streaks on the meat, and a rim to prevent oil spilling. It really is a development of the flat bakestone that used to be found in every Welsh household. The cast iron conducts and distributes heat evenly, producing a balanced cooking effect. A grillomat is not just for steaks. I use mine, which I purchased nearly thirty years ago, for bacon, lamb chops, vegetables, fish and fried bread! Grillomats are available from any good kitchen shop or department store.

Serves 4-6
4 x 350-500 g (12-16 oz) cuttlefish or squid
2 red peppers
2 yellow peppers
350 g (12 oz) large red onions
225 g (8 oz) potatoes
2 tablespoons olive oil
4 garlic cloves, crushed or coarsely chopped
salt and freshly ground black pepper
½ teaspoon oregano
½ teaspoon paprika
1 tablespoon wine vinegar

Prepare the cuttlefish, reserving the tentacles and ink sac for a stew. Cut the bodies of the cuttlefish into about 3 cm (1¼ in) squares, and the peppers and onions to about the same size. Cut the potatoes into 5 mm (¼ in) thick semi-circles. Heat some of the oil and fry the potatoes over a medium heat, until lightly brown and just soft. Add the garlic and cook for a few seconds. Season with salt and pepper, remove and reserve the potatoes.

Add the peppers to the pan skin side down, cover and fry until they just begin to char on the edges. Sprinkle with the oil, salt and pepper and oregano, remove from the pan and reserve. Do the same with the large pieces of onion.

Spread the cuttlefish in one layer in the pan and cook for 1-2 minutes on each side until just cooked through and cut easily with a table knife. Dust with paprika, salt and pepper then return all other vegetables and potatoes to the pan, carefully stir-frying to heat through. Drizzle with a little more oil, douse with vinegar, cover the pan and turn off the heat. Leave for 30-40 seconds then serve with a crisp green dressed salad.

Cuttlefish or Squid Stew

The ink of cuttlefish is very plentiful, rich and black. It is the defensive cloud the creature uses to confuse its prey. It has an unctuous richness and dramatic colour, greatly enhancing the flavour of the dish.

Serves 4
450 g (1 lb) cuttlefish or squid, trimmed, tentacles and ink sacs reserved
1 tablespoon oil
225 g (8 oz) onions, cut into 1 cm (½ in) half-rings
150 g (6 oz) head fennel, cut into 5 mm (¼ in) half-rings
4 garlic cloves, crushed and chopped
½ orange
300 ml (10 fl oz) red wine
225 g (8 oz) chopped tomatoes
1 tablespoon tomato purée
½ teaspoon paprika
salt and freshly ground black pepper

*W*ash the cuttlefish trimmings, reserving the ink. Ensure the beaks found at the centre of the tentacles are removed and the tiny suckers are washed out.

Heat a little oil and fry the onions quickly. Add the fennel and stir-fry together until just softening. Remove from the pan and reserve.

Add a little more oil and fry the cuttlefish pieces with the garlic for 1-2 minutes over a brisk heat. Return the vegetables to the pan and cook for 2-3 minutes. Squeeze in the orange juice, adding the peel in one piece, douse with half the wine and cook for several minutes. Add the tomatoes, tomato purée and paprika, cover and simmer gently for 5 minutes. Mix the remaining wine with the ink, add to the pan and cook for about 3 minutes. Check and adjust the seasoning. Serve with rice or couscous.

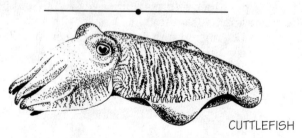

CUTTLEFISH

TARTLETS OF FRESH CRAB

Taffy Wooles at the Hollyland makes these simple yet tasty starters. The pastry gives an extra nutty flavour to the crab; the crème fraîche, made in Pembrokeshire, takes away some of the rich flavour.

Serves 4
450 g (1 lb) puff pastry
225 g (8 oz) brown crabmeat
dash of tabasco sauce
225 g (8 oz) white crabmeat
1 lemon, cut in half
225 g (8 oz) crème fraîche
½ teaspoon paprika
dressed green salad to serve

Pre-heat the oven to 200ºC / 400ºF / gas 6. Grease a baking sheet. Roll out the pastry and use a cutter to make into eight 5 cm (2 in) rounds. Arrange on the prepared baking tray, prick well with a fork and put in the fridge for 30 minutes. Bake in the pre-heated oven for 10-15 minutes until light golden. Leave to cool.

Lightly mash and season the brown meat with tabasco and the white meat with the juice of half the lemon. Place a 3 cm (1½ in) cutter on a pastry round then spoon in some of the white meat, pressing down gently. Top with some brown meat and finally some crème fraîche. Carefully remove the cutter so the crab is about 2 cm (1 in) high. Dust with paprika. Complete the other tartlets. Cut the remaining half-lemon into wedges and garnish the tartlets. Serve two each as a starter with dressed green salad.

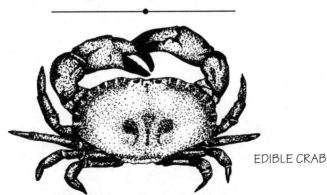

EDIBLE CRAB

MARINATED AND PICKLED MACKEREL

In August, many shoals of harvest mackerel chaff the seas around the coast in pursuit of their own offspring, whitebait. The small fish, only about 225 g (8 oz) at the largest, are very sweet, but must be gutted as they leave the sea. Ann at Jemima's wisely uses mackerel when they are plentiful in the summer, and cures some for the winter months in just the same way that they do with herrings in Scandinavia. Provided the fish are kept in the brine they will keep indefinitely in the fridge and you can use them as required.

Serves 6
15-20 mackerel
50 ml (2 fl oz) vinegar
225 g (8 oz) onions, sliced
brown bread to serve

FOR THE FIRST MARINADE
12 bay leaves
450 g (1 lb) sea salt
225 g (8 oz) sugar
15 g (½ oz) black peppercorns, crushed
15 g (½ oz) allspice berries, crushed

FOR THE SECOND MARINADE
225 g (8 oz) sugar
150 ml (5 fl oz) white wine vinegar
15 g (½ oz) whole black peppercorns
1 teaspoon whole pickling spice

First clean the fish, removing the heads, tails and insides, washing well and soaking for 30 minutes in water and the vinegar. Then remove the fish from the liquid and layer it head to tail in a plastic container with bay leaves and cover with the salt, sugar and spices. Leave for several days in the fridge for the brine to form, then lightly weigh down to ensure all the fish are covered, and store in the fridge.

To use the mackerel, remove as required from the brine, rinse and fillet the fish lengthways, taking out the central bone, and layer the fillets in a tray. Cover with onions. To make up the second marinade, simmer the ingredients for 5 minutes then allow to cool. Pour over the mackerel and chill for 5 days or longer. Then serve cold with brown bread.

MARINATED MACKEREL IN CIDER

We used to catch literally hundreds of mackerel in the summer from our boat at Langland Bay on the Gower peninsula, selling them to tourists for sixpence each (2½ British new pence), or three for a shilling (5 pence). With inflation, by the mid-seventies they were a shilling each or three for half-a-crown (12½ pence). This dish is a great way of using freshest mackerel so it will remain delicious for up to a week.

Serves 4-6
6 x 350 g (12 oz) fresh mackerel (or whatever size available)
1 tablespoon oil
600 ml (1 pint) strong farmhouse cider
50 ml (2 fl oz) cider or wine vinegar
50 g (2 oz) sugar
25 g (1 oz) salt
225 g (8 oz) onions, sliced
225 g (8 oz) cooking apples, cored and sliced
2 sprigs of fresh thyme or ½ teaspoon dried
12 black peppercorns
12 allspice berries
6 cloves

Fillet the mackerel to remove central bone and place skin-side down in an oiled, flameproof roasting tray, tightly packed in one layer. Simmer all other ingredients for 3-5 minutes, then spoon over the mackerel. Put the tray on the heat, shaking gently to ensure all the fish are separate, and just barely bring to a simmer, then switch off the heat and allow to cool. Press the fish gently below the juices, cover, and store in the fridge for up to a week. The juice will form a light jelly that is delicious to eat with the mackerel, together with a small salad.

Variation
Instead of using apples, you could substitute 2 pickled walnuts. Chop them roughly and add with 2 tablespoons of the black pickling vinegar instead of the cider or wine vinegar.

Scallops

Sometimes fishmongers will have the fresh queen scallops in their shells. They are about 5-7 cm (2-3 in) across the shell, compared to the king scallop which can be up to 15 cm (6 in) with much heavier shells. They are both swimming bi-valve (two-shell) shellfish that develop one hefty central muscle; it is probably the most succulent seafood of all, with a fine texture.

To remove scallops from their shells, insert a sharp knife from the side, cutting the muscle as close to the top flat shell as possible, then scoop from the deep shell, reserving this for presentation of the dish. In seaside pubs, these are frequently used as ashtrays as they are virtually unbreakable! The shells can be re-used if washed well and stored in a dry place.

The meat inside contains the main white muscle, to which the orange roe is attached, the liver and frill, which can be carefully pulled from the rest and discarded. Wash the meat quickly in cold water but never leave it to soak, even for a minute, as it will absorb water rapidly and become more flabby. This, of course, is one of the tricks of the trade, and most frozen scallops have been soaked to put on weight. It's a good way to sell water for a high price! If using frozen scallops, defrost them naturally and you will see the water you have paid for! These are, however, fine for most scallop recipes as they do retain the texture and flavour quite well.

——————————•——————————

Queen Scallops with Garlic and Coriander

This dish presents beautifully on individual shells, but if you can only buy the scallop meats, present in individual small gratin dishes. You can dredge the scallops with fresh breadcrumbs before grilling to give a crunchy top, but I prefer the natural soft texture of the scallops.

You can make the garlic butter and chill it for several hours, or it can be made in advance and will keep in the fridge for a week. I usually make double the quantity, split it into four and freeze some for later use. The advantage with this recipe is that it will spread directly from the chiller, but must always be kept cool. You can vary the recipe using different herbs according to the meat or fish you are cooking. Parsley butter is perfect with lighter fish, basil gives a more Mediterranean flavour, and coriander goes well with shellfish. The best extra virgin olive oil will enhance the flavour, and balsamic vinegar can replace the lemon juice for a more robust savoury tang. I have used fresh green chillies for zing, or just chervil for the most delicate taste of all. For a party you can make several different flavours and use for garlic bread with a difference!

Serves 4
36 queen scallops in the shell or 450 g (1 lb) king or queen scallop meats

FOR THE GARLIC AND CORIANDER BUTTER
2-3 garlic cloves
15 g (½ oz) fresh coriander, chopped
25 g (1 oz) spring onion, as green as possible, sliced
1 teaspoon dried or pickled green peppercorns, crushed
100 g (4 oz) lightly salted butter, cut into 8 pieces to soften
150 ml (5 fl oz) sunflower oil
juice of 1 lemon or 2 teaspoons white wine vinegar
crusty bread to serve

Remove the skin from the garlic by squashing it on a board with the flat of a heavy knife so the husk falls away. Put the cloves in a food processor with the coriander, spring onion and peppercorns and process for 10-15 seconds until quite finely chopped. Add the butter and blend for a further 15 seconds until smooth and green, cleaning the sides of the processor with a spatula. Slowly add the oil and lemon juice or wine vinegar then pour or scoop out into a container with a sealed lid and chill for 1 hour.

Pre-heat the oven to 200ºC/400ºF/gas 6, or pre-heat the grill to maximum. Put one queen scallop into each shell (or divide them between four individual dishes). If using kings, cut them into three slices. Put a teaspoon of garlic butter on to each scallop, place on a roasting tray and put into the pre-heated oven or under the grill for 4-5 minutes until the butter is sizzling and the scallops just hot through but not overcooked, as they will quickly shrivel and toughen. Serve immediately with lots of bread to mop up the butter.

————————●————————

SMOKED SALMON

*T*he art or craft of smoking salmon dates back centuries. Salmon is first salted or brined, then infused with cool smoke to flavour and preserve the fish, just as hams are cured. Naturally, more salt and longer smoking makes a heavier 'cure' that will keep longer. Indian tribes on the Pacific coast used to smoke salmon to store it for winter months. As the process was refined for the most aristocratic tables in the country, the cures became lighter and more delicate. The best smoked salmon has a good hint of oak smoke without any burnt or kippery flavour.

The finest smoked salmon undoubtedly comes from the large spring fish that are caught on the Wye from February to May. These fish have a very high fat content which provides the succulence and flavour, and they give thick sides of salmon that can be flavoured from the smoke without drying out the flesh. In the same way a large roast of beef has the most succulence and flavour compared to a smaller joint which dries out before the outer flavours reach their peak. A small salmon that has been in the river a while (such as the one I caught at Wyesham) will have lost any fat and will only give a very thin side of salmon. It is best to return it to the river as we did!

Farmed salmon are smoked and often small sides are sold very reasonably. These are quite good, but the cure tends to be very light and the fish highly perishable, so use it up quickly. Nothing will compare in flavour with a large smoked springer!

A great innovation that actually goes back to the Indian-style is when the fish is cured in hot smoke which actually cooks the fish, just as is done when smoking mackerel. Ex-rugby player Pat Daniels does this at his smokery in Glamorgan. Hot-smoked salmon steaks have a very distinctive oaky flavour, yet retain a succulence from the oiliness of the fish. Hot-smoked salmon is delicious cold or can be re-heated carefully – it is actually best 'simmered in the bag' for a few minutes to heat without drying.

HOT-SMOKED SALMON WITH SAUCE VIÈRGE

This dish is quick, easy and quite superb! Supermarkets have caught up the success of local smokeries and now hot-cured steaks are readily available from most major stores. Best of all, they are cured as modern steaks from the side of fish, and hence have no bones. A quick version of this dish can be made by substituting 2 teaspoons of pesto sauce for the fresh basil and passata. It is still delicious! A similar, less expensive meal can be made using hot-smoked mackerel, kipper fillets or smoked cod, haddock or even whiting.

Serves 4
450 g (1 lb) small new potatoes
4 x 100 g (4 oz) hot-smoked salmon steaks
1 bowl of mixed salad leaves

FOR THE SALAD DRESSING
1 tablespoon extra virgin olive oil
juice of ½ lemon

FOR THE SAUCE
1 bunch of fresh basil, stalks removed and reserved and leaves finely chopped
3 tablespoons extra virgin olive oil
½ teaspoon mustard
1 teaspoon balsamic vinegar
salt and freshly ground black pepper
150 ml (5 fl oz) fresh tomato juice or passata

Put the potatoes to boil in lightly salted water with the basil stalks and simmer for 10-15 minutes until just soft, so that a knife penetrates them easily. You can heat the salmon in the same pan, putting the steaks on a plate on top to warm through for a minute. Drain.

Mix together the oil and lemon juice and use to dress the salad leaves.

Mix the chopped basil leaves with the remaining sauce ingredients and serve on the side with the hot-smoked salmon, new potatoes and salad.

————————————•————————————

PRAWNS

In the summer and autumn, you can catch prawns in rock pools all around the Welsh coastline. The best time is at the lowest tides of all, when they are confined in pools and gullies as the tide recedes. In many bays and estuaries they can be caught on the sand in shallow water with a large push net.
The most famous character of all, around the turn of the century, was the blind fisherman of Mumbles, who netted prawns with great success, and whose portrait, complete with net, still hangs in the Glyn Vivian Art Gallery in Swansea.
Nothing compares with the flavour of fresh prawns cooked for seconds in boiling sea water. Trace elements give them a distinctive colour and flavour that is impossible to recreate. Many times we gorged endless pints of prawns freshly netted from Rhossili Bay and cooked on the sea shore itself, washed down with endless pints of scrumpy which was our tipple in the fishing hut at Kitchen Corner, a most aptly named landmark.

PRAWN COCKTAIL WITH GINGER AND SESAME

You can buy frozen prawns anywhere, and if defrosted naturally these have a good sweet flavour. Never soak them in water to defrost them or you will wash away the best flavours. Whole prawns in the shell have an excellent flavour and are good value provided you have the patience to peel them. You can use the shells and heads for a seafood soup or prawn bisque and eat the tails in a delicious salad or cocktail. This recipe is a prawn cocktail with a difference, but using ingredients that are readily available. You could add some freshly chopped coriander or basil to the marinade for an additional turn of flavour.

Serves 4
675 g (1½ lb) prawns in their shells
1 heaped teaspoon freshly grated ginger root
2 teaspoons sesame oil
juice and grated zest of 1 lemon
dash of tabasco sauce
2 tablespoons good quality French mayonnaise
1 teaspoon sun-dried tomato paste or tomato purée
4 leaves of crisp lettuce, Cos, Webbs or iceberg, shredded
2 sprigs of fresh parsley, chopped
lemon wedges

*D*e-shell the prawns by separating the heads and peeling off the tail segments. Reserve the shells for soup. Do not rinse the prawns. Mix together the ginger, sesame oil and juice of the lemon with a little of the zest and the tabasco. Marinate the prawns in this mixture for up to 20 minutes as you make the rest of the dish.

Mix together the mayonnaise and tomato paste or purée. Arrange the salad leaves in individual bowls then drizzle some of the marinade juice over the lettuce. Cover with prawns and mix the remaining juice and ginger with the mayonnaise. Spoon on to the prawns. Garnish with freshly chopped parsley and small lemon wedges to serve.

SMOKED MACKEREL PÂTÉ

*H*ot-smoked fish are very easy to use for pâté. For this recipe, I use smoked mackerel, Arbroath Smokie (haddock), buckling (herring), trout and salmon (hot-smoked or oaked). Canned fish such as sardines and salmon, or fish roe, particularly cod's roe, also make a good fish pâté. This recipe can be varied according to the fish used, but all tend to be rich and oily, so the use of curd cheese makes a good contrast as its astringent flavour cuts through the oiliness. Serve this style of pâté with hot toast, bread, pitta, focaccia, crudités (sticks of raw vegetables) or salad.

Serves 4-6
450 g (1 lb) smoked mackerel, skinned and boned
225 g (8 oz) low-fat curd or cream cheese
50 g (2 oz) fresh wholemeal breadcrumbs
teaspoon mixed freshly ground black pepper and cayenne
juice of ½ lemon or 2 teaspoons white wine vinegar

*M*ake sure the fish is free of skin and bones. Scrape off any fat from the skin. There may be a few bones towards the centre of the thickest part of the fish and in the belly. Some small fins from around the side can easily be pulled away. Flake the fish flesh with your fingers and you will feel any other bones.

Fork the fish in a bowl or pound in a food processor for a few seconds. Mix in the curd or cream cheese and breadcrumbs to a smooth paste. Season with pepper and cayenne and add the lemon juice or wine vinegar. Put into individual ramekins or in a larger pâté dish. Chill for at least 1 hour, preferably overnight, before serving.

Variations
Other fish will all have their own individual flavours and can be treated in a similar way. Interesting variations of flavour can be obtained by adding any of the following to a quarter of the mixture:

2 teaspoons horseradish sauce
25 g (1 oz) laverbread
2 teaspoons sun-dried tomato paste or tomato purée
2 teaspoons chilli sauce
2 teaspoons mustard

You can also use smoked meat, particularly chicken, or cooked smoked haddock, but you will need to process the meat in a food processor and add about 25 g (1 oz) of butter to smooth the mixture.

Taramasalata can be made to the same recipe, using smoked cod's roe and incorporating 250 ml (8 fl oz) of olive oil and extra lemon juice. Again, this is best done in a food processor. A cunning extra addition is 1-2 teaspoons of barbecue smoke flavouring, in which case you can use tinned roe.

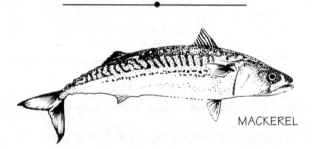

MACKEREL

STARTERS - MEAT

BLACK PUDDING WITH MUSTARD AND APPLES

This combination makes a wonderful starter, with the sharp flavour of the apples contrasting with the rich black pudding and the tart sauce.

Serves 4
450 g (1 lb) black pudding
1 tablespoon oil
100 g (4 oz) smoked streaky bacon, rinded
225 g (8 oz) onions, sliced
225 g (8 oz) cooking apples, cored, peeled, sliced
salt and freshly ground black pepper

FOR THE SAUCE
2 teaspoons Dijon mustard
1 teaspoon walnut oil
1 teaspoon cider or wine vinegar
1 tablespoon water

Pre-heat the grill or oven to 200ºC/400ºF/gas 6. Cut the pudding into diagonal 1 cm (1/2 in) slices. Heat the oil and fry the pudding for a minute on each side. Put into a flameproof roasting tray. Cut the bacon into 2 cm (1 in) pieces and fry until crisp and the fat quite gold. Put on to the pudding. Fry the onions in the bacon fat until just turning slightly gold on the edges. Add the apples, cover and cook for 1-2 minutes until soft. Season with salt and pepper and spoon over the black pudding. Put under the pre-heated grill or in the oven for 5 minutes to heat through well.

Meanwhile, put the sauce ingredients in a screw-top jar, shake well and serve with the hot pudding.

SPICY SAUSAGE WITH LENTILS AND TAPENADE

*I*ncreasingly, Welsh butchers are striving to produce good quality sausages, not only for grilling but for boiling or salami in true continental tradition. There is now even a Welsh sausage championship every year at the Royal Welsh Show! Any boiling sausage will do for this starter, but the best of all would be Italian Zampone sausage made in a pig's trotter, which is rich with deep flavour. It is also quite expensive. To give lentils a really good, deep flavour, the standard aromats and a stock are far better than plain water. You could make a similar recipe substituting confit of duck or goose, using the fat for cooking the aromats with the lentils (see *Crispy Leg of Duck with Lentils and Turnips* page 118).

Serves 4
1 tablespoon oil
100 g (4 oz) onions, diced
100 g (4 oz) carrots, diced
50 g (2 oz) celery, diced
2 garlic cloves, crushed
225 g (8 oz) green or puy lentils
150 ml (5 fl oz) full red wine such as Merlot
300 ml (10 fl oz) chicken stock
350 g (12 oz) boiling sausage
salt and freshly ground black pepper

FOR THE GARNISH
2 tablespoons olive oil
4 thin slices wholemeal bread, cut into triangles
2 teaspoons black olive paste (tapenade)
1 teaspoon anchovy essence or sauce

FOR THE SAUCE
1 heaped teaspoon English mustard
1 teaspoon pesto sauce
1 tablespoon olive oil
50 ml (2 fl oz) dry white wine or water

*H*eat the oil and fry the onions, carrots and celery until just browning slightly on the edges. Add the garlic, husk and all, then add the lentils and fry for 2 minutes, stirring continuously. Douse with wine and continue cooking for 1 minute to evaporate at least half the liquid, then pour in the stock and bring to a simmer. Cover and simmer for 30 minutes, stirring occasionally and topping up the juice to cover the lentils as they plump up. When the lentils are soft, add the sausage, heat through thoroughly and season with salt and pepper.

Meanwhile, heat the oil and fry the bread to make crispy triangles. Mix together the olive paste and anchovy essence and spread on the bread. Put all the sauce ingredients into a screw-top jar and shake well to mix.

Slice the sausage into 1 cm ($^{1}/_{2}$ in) diagonal rings. Spoon the lentils on to warmed serving plates, top with the sausage and garnish with the fried bread triangles. Pour the mustard sauce around and serve immediately.

SMOKED TURKEY WITH CRUNCHY SALAD AND PICKLED WALNUT DRESSING

Pickled walnuts are a great thing to use at Christmas with all the cold meats, particularly with cold turkey stuffing. This dish can be made with cold roast turkey, but is also good with just a few slices of cold smoked turkey or smoked chicken.

Serves 4
225 g (8 oz) sliced smoked turkey
225 g (8 oz) mouli radish
a large bowl of mixed salad leaves

FOR THE DRESSING
150 ml (5 fl oz) virgin olive oil
1 teaspoon mustard
salt and freshly ground black pepper
2 tablespoons vinegar from the pickled walnuts
1 whole pickled walnut, chopped

Cut the turkey slices into long, thin strips and the mouli into 3 mm ($^{1}/_{8}$ in) rings. Use a little of the dressing oil and toss the salad to coat well. Arrange the mouli slices on the salad with the turkey strips on top.

Put all the dressing ingredients into a screw-top jar and shake for a few seconds to make a thick sauce. Spoon the chunky parts over the centre of each plate and drizzle the rest over the leaves.

COUNTRY PÂTÉ

This is a good standard pâté. It can be made more elaborate by adding other meat, particularly game, flavourings such as wild mushrooms, and herbs from tarragon to coriander. It takes a while to make but is great for a party as it will only improve if made a few days in advance. Serve it with French bread or ciabatta and some *Beetroot and Onion Relish* or *Light Marrow Chutney* (see page 172).

Serves 12
450 g (1 lb) belly pork, skinned, boned and cut into 2.5 cm (1 in) cubes

FOR THE MARINADE
225 g (8 oz) carrots, chopped
225 g (8 oz) celery, chopped
225 g (8 oz) shallots or onions, chopped
4 garlic cloves, chopped
2 tablespoons oil
150 ml (5 fl oz) fruity red wine
salt and freshly ground black pepper
4 sprigs of fresh sage or 1 teaspoon dried sage

1 tablespoon oil
225 g (8 oz) chicken livers
100 g (4 oz) shallots, finely chopped
50 ml (2 fl oz) brandy
50 ml (2 fl oz) port
1 teaspoon green peppercorns, crushed
50 g (2 oz) fresh breadcrumbs
1 heaped teaspoon chopped fresh parsley
50 g (2 oz) curd cheese
1 egg
225 g (8 oz) streaky bacon, rinded and thinly sliced

To get real flavour, you need to marinate the pork for several days. Mix together the marinade ingredients, pour over the pork and chill for up to 3 days, mixing several times. Remove the meat and drain off the juices from the vegetables and reserve both separately.

Fry the marinated vegetables in a little oil until softened (this can be done in a microwave), then cool. Finely chop them in a food processor then add the pork, taking care not to curdle the fat by over-processing.

Drain the juice off the livers and chop roughly. Meanwhile, fry the shallots in a little oil until light golden. Add the livers and cook quickly for 1 minute then pour in the brandy, which will ignite with the heat, so take care! Add the port and leave to cool. Remove the livers with a slotted spoon and chop more finely to about 3 mm ($^1/_8$ in). Add this with the shallots and liquor to the pork mixture, together with the peppercorns, breadcrumbs and parsley.

Mix together the curd cheese and egg in a food processor and add to the meat mixture already in the bowl. Add the marinade juices, mixing with a large spoon until all the ingredients are well blended. It should be a thick but just flowing mixture. Season with salt and pepper. Test the seasoning by putting a dessertspoon of the mixture on a plate and cooking for a few minutes in the oven, or a few seconds in the microwave. Taste this for flavour and seasoning.

Lightly oil a 30 cm (12 in) pâté terrine. Line the terrine with the bacon, covering just the bottom or the bottom and sides if you prefer, ensuring that the corners are well pressed down. Fill to 1 cm ($^1/_2$ in) from the top with the pâté mixture then cover with a layer of bacon. Cover the terrine with the lid or foil and chill for 3-4 hours.

Pre-heat the oven to 180ºC/350ºF/gas 4. Fill a roasting tray with 2.5 cm (1 in) of hot water, stand the terrine in this and cook in the pre-heated oven for 65-75 minutes. Test by inserting a knife in the centre; it should emerge clean and hot. If not, cook for a little longer.

Allow the pâté to cool for 10 minutes then, ideally using another terrine laid over the top, lightly press to remove any trapped air, and leave a weight on top until the pâté is cold. The pâté should be refrigerated for at least 48 hours before serving.

Serve the pâté directly from the terrine. Once the first slice has been scooped out, the rest will cut easily from the terrine. You can remove it in one by sliding a thin knife around the edges and half immersing the terrine in hot water for a few seconds. The pâté will drop out when inverted and can then be cut into 2.5 cm (1 in) slices and arranged on a platter. Chill until it is served.

———————————●———————————

CARMARTHEN HAM IN BEER

*T*his is a good recipe for a publican who has plenty of ullage beer, which is perfect for this dish. Use this instead of the water. Also try using this beer to make the *Beer Chutney* (see page 171) to serve with this dish.

Serves 6-8
1 x 1.5 kg (3 lb) chunk of ham for boiling
450 g (1 lb) onions, roughly chopped
100 g (4 oz) carrots, chopped
100 g (4 oz) celery, chopped
12 black peppercorns
12 cloves
100 g (4 oz) dark muscovado sugar
4 bay leaves
1 large sprig of fresh lovage or thyme
1.2 litres (2 pints) bitter beer
about 600 ml (1 pint) water

*P*ut all the ingredients into a large pan, adding enough water to cover the ham completely. Bring to the boil then lower the heat and simmer for 1 hour, topping up the liquid with more beer or water as necessary. If a larger chunk of ham is used, cook for a further 10 minutes for each extra 450 g (1 lb). Leave the ham to cool in the liquid until cold then chill for at least 24 hours before removing from the jelly. Slice thinly and serve with home-made pickles and new potatoes or chips if serving as a main course.

ORGANIC CARROTS

SMOKED CHICKEN RISOTTO

The light smoked flavour with the rice makes a good combination with vegetables without being overpowering. You will need about half a smoked chicken. Arborio is the most common type of risotto rice, and you will find this in all good supermarkets.

Serves 4
450 g (1 lb) smoked chicken
600 ml (1 pint) water
1 tablespoon olive oil
1 red pepper, diced
225 g (8 oz) red onions, diced
100 g (4 oz) carrots, diagonally sliced
225 g (8 oz) risotto rice
100 ml (4 fl oz) dry sherry
2 large sprigs of fresh parsley, chopped
100 g (4 oz) Parmesan, Pecorino or Cheddar, freshly grated

Pull the chicken meat away from the skin and bones and roughly chop it. Use the skin and bones with the water and vegetable trimmings to make a stock. Place them all in a large pan, bring to the boil and simmer for about 20 minutes, topping up if necessary to make about 450 ml (15 fl oz) of stock. Strain the stock, discard the bones and keep the stock hot.

Heat the oil and fry the pepper, onions and carrots until softening and lightly browning on the edges. Add the rice and stir together for 1-2 minutes to absorb the flavours, then pour in the hot stock, bring to a simmer and simmer for 5 minutes. Add the chopped meat, stirring occasionally for a further 10 minutes, by which time the rice should be just softening and almost ready. Add the sherry, mixing well, then add the parsley. The risotto should have a little liquid remaining. Cover, switch off the heat and leave for 5 minutes. Serve with freshly grated cheese.

STARTERS - VEGETARIAN

CHARGRILLED VEGETABLES WITH CITRUS DRESSING

Cooking vegetables on an open fire or on direct heat almost disappeared when cheap pots and pans became available. It is less messy to boil vegetables, but in many cases the flavour is thrown out with the water. As vegetables cook, the juices, acidity and sugars change. If concentrated, they will eventually turn dark with a caramelized flavour. This is what we aim to achieve by charring vegetables. But many are best when the texture is still crisp, so it is a fine balance to produce the unctuous caramel richness of burnt sweetness, while retaining a certain firm and fresh flavour.

With the increasing use of barbecues and grillomats, this style of vegetable cooking is again becoming more popular. It is reminiscent of the smell of charcoal across a Mediterranean beach drenched from the heat of the sun, and the heady aroma of citrus blossom. Citrus enlivens the taste buds which are otherwise quelled by the sugars from the caramel juices. This dish can be a vegetarian starter or main course, or an accompaniment to grilled or roasted meat or fish.

Serves 4
1 red pepper
1 green pepper
1 yellow pepper
1 aubergine
4 x 15 cm (6 in) courgettes
4 x 50 g (2 oz) red onions
1 small bunch of fresh parsley
1 small bunch of fresh sage
1 small bunch of fresh rosemary
1 small bunch of fresh thyme
4 tablespoons olive oil
salt and freshly ground black pepper
1 lemon
1 lime
1 small grapefruit
1 teaspoon mustard

Pre-heat a chargrill, grillomat or grill. Cut the peppers into quarters lengthways, removing the seeds. Cut the aubergine into 2 cm ($^3/_4$ in) rings, the courgettes into halves lengthways, and the onions into halves then across into rings. Trim the herbs, reserving the most succulent leaves for the dressing. Roughly chop the remainder and add to a little of the olive oil with some salt and pepper and a dash of lemon juice. Coat the vegetables with this dressing.

When the grill is just beginning to smoke, place the vegetables on to it and grill over a brisk heat until they are charring well on the outsides. Baste with extra dressing, then arrange on a warmed serving tray, season with salt and pepper and grate some of the citrus zest over vegetables. Keep warm.

To make the citrus dressing, squeeze the lemon, lime and grapefruit, combining the juices with a little of their grated zest in a screw-top jar. Add the mustard and remaining oil, close tightly, then shake to form a thick, velvety sauce. Drizzle a little over the vegetables and serve the remainder separately.

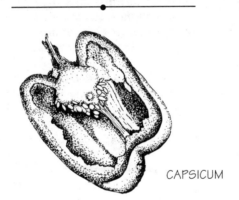

CAPSICUM

PIEDMONTESE PEPPERS WITH A RICH STUFFING

*F*ranco Taruschio popularized this pepper dish in his restaurant, The Walnut Tree in Abergavenny. Now many contemporary chefs and writers have followed his recipe. This is a variation on the theme. The key to success is to make the little boats from the peppers which will contain and mingle the flavours within. The dramatic shape and colour of the red peppers is enhanced by the bulbous, round, plump plum tomatoes. This is a vegan version that concentrates many flavours, making it suitable as an appetizer or main course, or it can be served as an accompaniment to roast or grilled meat, poultry or fish.

Serves 4
4 large red peppers
4 large fresh plum tomatoes or 8 tinned tomatoes
8 sun-dried tomatoes in oil
1 large bunch of fresh basil
25 g (1 oz) pine kernels
8 fat garlic cloves, chopped
4 tablespoons extra virgin olive oil
salt and freshly ground black pepper
225 g (8 oz) roughly chopped onion, carrot and celery
600 ml (1 pint) water

*P*re-heat the oven to 220ºC/425ºF/gas 7. Halve the peppers lengthways, cutting through the stalk, and carefully remove the seeds and pith to retain a shallow cup shape. Skin the tomatoes by plunging them into boiling water for 20-30 seconds until the skin begins to split, then remove and slide off the skins. Cut the tomatoes in half lengthways, removing the stalk mark. Using kitchen scissors, snip half the sun-dried tomatoes into very thin strips and reserve. Roughly snip the remainder and combine with the basil leaves, pine kernels and garlic in a food processor, and process with a little oil and salt and pepper to form a paste. Put this into the pepper halves and top each half with a half-tomato, rounded side uppermost.

Put the chopped onion, carrot and celery in a roasting tray and arrange the peppers on top so they will not fall over. Add about a pint of hot water to steam peppers during cooking. Pour the remaining oil into each pepper, top with the snipped sun-dried tomatoes, give a final seasoning and cover with foil. Cook in the pre-heated oven for 20-30 minutes until they are just soft but not collapsing, retaining all the juices in each half-pepper. Serve hot or cold.

———————————•———————————

ℬAKED AUBERGINE WITH PESTO AND TOMATO SAUCE

𝒜ubergines have a wonderful silky texture when cooked, but a horrible
sponginess that will absorb every nasty flavour if half raw, as I've experienced
with ratatouille made by amateurs in numerous restaurants. I also like the
crunch, colour and contrasting flavour of the skin.
Many cooks are put off aubergines by the laborious preparation of salting and
soaking that is so often recommended. Forget it! Follow this very simple recipe
and the result is delicious. I often prepare a tray of these, store them in the
fridge and re-heat when needed in the microwave.

Serves 4
2 x 225 g (8 oz) aubergines
2 tablespoons olive oil
2 tablespoons pesto sauce
450 g (1 lb) ripe tomatoes
1 shallot, finely chopped
1 sprig of fresh parsley, finely chopped
1 sprig of fresh thyme, finely chopped
1 sprig of fresh fennel, finely chopped
2 tablespoons extra virgin olive oil
1 tablespoon balsamic vinegar
salt and freshly ground black pepper

𝒫re-heat the oven to 200ºC/400ºF/gas 6. Cut the aubergines into 2 cm (³/₄ in)
rings. Place on a roasting tray with the oil and coat both sides of each piece.
Bake in the pre-heated oven for 15 minutes until golden on top and soft, so a
knife will drop through the flesh with no resistance. Top each piece with pesto,
and lower the oven temperature to cool: 110ºC/ 225ºF/gas ¹/₄.

Liquidize and sieve the tomatoes to give a smooth sauce. Add the shallot
and herbs and transfer to a pan. Bring to a simmer then cook for 2-3 minutes.
Allow to cool slightly then whisk in the extra virgin olive oil and balsamic
vinegar. Check and adjust the seasoning, and serve on a plate topped with
the aubergines.

PUMPKIN MASH

The pumpkin family includes squashes, gourds and marrows of all descriptions. These can be treated similarly in the culinary world, although there is a surprising variation in flavour and texture from different varieties. They all contain a lot of water and fibre, so you have to judge the elements of these two factors when cooking – so often people will boil pumpkin flesh, which only dilutes its flavour. For most dishes, I start by baking them to concentrate the juices and intensify the nuances, which can vary from a green vegetable to a rich nutty flavour.

Autumn is the main season for marrows and pumpkins, but imported ones are now found all year round, not just at Halloween. Just think of the tons of pumpkin that are discarded after being carved into a mask for Halloween! What a waste of delicious vegetables.

Serves 4
1 kg (2 lb) pumpkin or marrow
2 tablespoons oil
225 g (8 oz) mixed onion, carrot and celery, cut into 2 cm (1/2 in) dice
2 garlic cloves, crushed
1 teaspoon dried basil or tarragon
350 g (12 oz) tomatoes, chopped
salt and freshly ground black pepper

Pre-heat the oven to 200ºC/400ºF/gas 6. Cut the pumpkin or marrow in half and bake in the pre-heated oven for 30 minutes or until soft. Scoop out and discard the seeds then cut the soft pulp away from the skin.

Heat the oil and fry the vegetables until beginning to colour. Add the pumpkin, garlic, basil and tomatoes. Season with salt and pepper and simmer for 20 minutes, stirring frequently.

————————●————————

PASTA WITH CELERY AND BLUE CHEESE SAUCE

Pasta is a wonderful vehicle for all kinds of flavours, and this combination of celery with Blue Caerphilly or Stilton, mustard and port gives a rich, textured sauce which is quite delicious. This dish can also be served as a main course for two people.

Serves 4
225 g (8 oz) penne pasta, three-coloured if possible
salt and freshly ground black pepper
1 tablespoon oil
4 celery sticks, cut diagonally into 5 mm (1/4 in) slices
150 ml (5 fl oz) dry white wine
100 g (4 oz) Blue Caerphilly, Stilton or any other blue cheese, grated
2 teaspoons Dijon mustard
50 ml (2 fl oz) port

Cook the pasta in plenty of boiling salted water, as directed on the packet, until just firm. Drain, toss in a little oil and season with pepper.

Meanwhile, heat the oil, add the celery, cover and fry for 3-4 minutes to soften, stirring well to stop it browning. Season with salt and pepper, add the wine and cook for a further 1-2 minutes. Using a slotted spoon, lift out the celery and add to the pasta in a bowl, mixing it in carefully.

Increase heat under the pan, add the cheese and stir until melted, then add the mustard and port and heat through. Pour over the pasta and serve.

SEABEET MOUSSE WITH TOMATO SAUCE

Seabeet grows on salt marshes around the high spring tide mark. It looks like old-fashioned spinach, dark green with big waxy leaves, but usually has gone to seed. If young plants with tender leaves are found they are delicious, otherwise just use spinach.

Serves 4-6
225 g (8 oz) seabeet or spinach leaves, stalks removed
100 g (4 oz) low-fat curd cheese
1 egg
½ teaspoon paprika
pinch of freshly grated nutmeg
salt and freshly ground black pepper
150 ml (5 fl oz) fresh tomato purée or passata
2 tablespoons extra virgin olive oil
1 teaspoon mustard

Pre-heat the oven to 190ºC/375ºF/gas 5, or use a microwave. Lightly oil four ramekins. Cook the seabeet or spinach in a covered pan with a minimum of water for a few minutes, until it has wilted. Drain, press lightly dry and leave to cool.

Put the seabeet or spinach in a food processor or bowl and mix with the cheese and egg until smooth. Add the spices and season with salt and pepper. Spoon the mixture into the ramekins to 1 cm (½ in) from the top. Either cook in the pre-heated oven for 10-15 minutes, or microwave on high for 2-3 minutes until set. Leave to stand for 1 minute.

Mix the tomato purée or passata, oil and mustard in a screw-top jar, shaking well to form a smooth sauce. Season to taste with salt and pepper. Run a knife round the edges of the ramekins then unmould them on to individual plates, surround with the sauce and serve. You can heat the sauce in the microwave to warm it if you wish.

———————————•———————————

BROAD BEAN, POTATO AND VEGETABLE RISOTTO

*T*his risotto has very tiny potatoes and young broad beans for sweetness and nutty flavour. Small broad beans can be eaten in their pods, cut as stick beans to 2 cm (1 in) pieces and lightly boiled. The smallest new potatoes are worth seeking out when absolutely fresh, just lifted from the ground.

Serves 4
225 g (8 oz) small new potatoes
100 g (4 oz) baby broad beans
1 tablespoon olive oil
225 g (8 oz) shallots, roughly chopped
100 g (4 oz) small carrots, sliced
2 garlic cloves, crushed
100 g (4 oz) arborio or other risotto rice
1 sprig of fresh thyme or savory, or ½ teaspoon of dried
100 g (4 oz) bacon, rinded and chopped
50 g (2 oz) butter
3 tablespoons cream
salt and freshly ground black pepper
50 g (2 oz) Cheddar or Pecorino, grated

*C*ook the potatoes in lightly salted water until just tender, then remove. Blanch beans in the same water, remove and reserve the vegetables and cooking liquor. Make this up to 300 ml (10 fl oz) with water if necessary.

*H*eat the oil and fry the shallots and carrots until just soft and turning gold at the edges. Add the garlic and rice and cook together briskly for several minutes. Pour in the vegetable cooking liquor and herbs, stirring continuously for 5 minutes. Add the potatoes and beans with the bacon pieces and butter. Simmer for 5-7 minutes, stirring frequently, keeping the rice very moist. When the rice is just cooked through, add the cream, stirring well. Season with salt and pepper and serve with grated cheese.

———————————●———————————

STARTERS - SOUPS

COCKLE CHOWDER

Cockles are the small clams that have been raked from estuaries of Wales for centuries. Fresh cockles should be soaked in a bowl of lightly salted water for 24 hours so that they clean themselves naturally. A spoonful of wholemeal flour or oatmeal in the water assists the purging process. Cockles in their shells are particularly good for this recipe, which needs as much juice as possible.

Serves 4-6
1.5 kg (3 lb) cockles in the shell or 450 g (1 lb) ready cooked cockles
100 g (4 oz) unsmoked streaky bacon, rinded
1 tablespoon oil
225 g (8 oz) onions
150 ml (5 fl oz) dry white wine or cider
1 sprig of fresh thyme or $\frac{1}{2}$ teaspoon dried thyme
100 g (4 oz) carrots, thinly sliced
450 g (1 lb) potatoes, peeled and diced
100 g (4 oz) leeks or spring onions, thinly sliced
300 ml (10 fl oz) milk
$\frac{1}{2}$ teaspoon cayenne pepper
1 small bunch of fresh parsley, chopped
salt and freshly ground black pepper

After the cockles have been soaking, wash them well in cold water and drain. Fry the bacon in a little oil until crisp but not brown, then remove from the pan. Chop half the onions and sauté in the bacon juice for about 2 minutes to soften. Add the wine or cider and thyme and cook for about 1 minute. Add all the cockles, cover the pan and increase the heat, shaking the pan for 3-4 minutes until all the shells are wide open and the cockles look bright and yellow on the 'tongue'. Leave to cool with the lid on.

Dice the remaining onion and fry in a little oil with the carrots and potatoes until softened. Shake the shells from the cockles, reserving all the juices. Add the juice from the cockles to the vegetables and simmer for 10-15 minutes until they are just tender.

Add the leeks or spring onions and simmer for 1 minute, then add the milk, cockles, bacon pieces, cayenne and chopped parsley. Heat through, check and adjust the seasoning and serve.

HEN CRAB SOUP

In the lobster and crab season, hen crabs are very cheap and many families who make dressed crab have a surfeit of the dark meat. It makes a delicious, rich soup, which can serve as a base for a fish casserole.

Serves 6-8
2 tablespoons oil
25 g (1 oz) butter
225 g (8 oz) onions, roughly chopped
100 g (4 oz) red pepper, roughly chopped
225 g (8 oz) brown hen crabmeat
100 g (4 oz) white crabmeat
1 bouquet garni (a strip of orange peel, a sprig of fresh thyme, a sprig of fresh parsley and a bay leaf, tied together)
200 ml (7 fl oz) dry white wine
450 g (1 lb) tin chopped tomatoes
600 ml (1 pint) light fish or chicken stock
½ teaspoon paprika
salt and freshly ground black pepper
150 ml (5 fl oz) cream
1 tablespoon chopped fresh parsley

Heat the oil and butter and fry the onions and pepper gently until softening but not colouring. Add the brown and half the white crabmeat and the bouquet garni, and cook for 1-2 minutes. Douse with wine and mix well. Add the tomatoes and stock, then season with paprika, salt and pepper and simmer for 10 minutes, stirring frequently. Allow to cool and remove the bouquet garni.

Liquidize the soup, then sieve it to give a smooth, thick texture. Return the soup to the pan and re-heat gently, adding the cream. Flake in the remaining white crabmeat, sprinkle with chopped parsley, dust with a little more paprika and serve.

WELSH CAWL

Welsh cawl is a good old traditional broth made from meat, root vegetables, herbs and leeks. The meat can be either lamb, beef or ham, but use the cheapest cuts: neck, shin, hock. Apart from onions, the root vegetables can vary, but are usually swede, carrot, turnip or parsnip. All these are chopped up and simmered with lots of water, seasoning and herbs to cook off any fattiness and leave the meat very tender, actually falling apart from the bone. Traditionally, the broth was always left to cool overnight so the fat would solidify and could be removed. When re-heated, generous amounts of freshly chopped leeks would be added to bring a lively flavour and colour. Arguments over what constitutes a traditional cawl are as futile as those relating to a *bouillabaisse*. They are just cheap peasant dishes which, when made with care, are utterly delicious.

QUICK LAMB CAWL

The name for this dish is 'cawl mamgu' – granny's broth. This is an easy version using familiar ingredients that retain their freshness in a quick cooking process.

Serves 6-8
900 g (2 lb) half shoulder lamb
450 g (1 lb) onions
225 g (8 oz) carrots
225 g (8 oz) turnips or parsnips
225 g (8 oz) swede
1 celery stick
2 teaspoons oil
2 garlic cloves, crushed
2 sprigs of fresh thyme or ½ teaspoon dried thyme
300 ml (10 fl oz) beer or cider
salt and freshly ground black pepper
450 g (1 lb) leeks
25 g (1 oz) fresh parsley, chopped

Cut the meat from the bone and slice into 1 cm (½ in) strips. Chop the bones and boil with about 2 litres (3½ pints) of water for 1 hour to make a stock. Trim all vegetables except the leeks and garlic and add the trimmings to the stock. Cut them into 2-3 cm (½-1 in) pieces and fry in the oil in a covered pan, stirring for 5 minutes until they begin to soften. Remove and add the diced meat to the pan and stir-fry on a brisk heat for 2-3 minutes. Add the crushed garlic, thyme and beer or cider, cover and cook for 1-2 minutes. Season with salt and pepper then return the vegetables to the pan, cover with the stock and simmer for 15 minutes until the vegetables and lamb are just cooked.

Cut the leeks lengthways into quarters, wash to remove any grit, then cut the whites into 2 cm (1 in) pieces. Add to the cawl and cook for 5 minutes or until all the vegetables and meat are tender. Finely slice the green of the leeks across the grain, not lengthways, add to the pan and bring to the boil. Check and adjust the seasoning and add a generous amount of parsley. Serve very hot.

CAWL CENNIN

*T*his broth is a very simple soup of stock and potatoes with leeks added as the authentic flavour. It was a good soup to make when lamb was too expensive and bones were cheap. It can be made as a vegetarian soup. The up-market version, famed in the great kitchens of the culinary world, is vichyssoise, made by pounding or liquidizing all the ingredients.

Serves 4-6
2 teaspoons oil
225 g (8 oz) onions or shallots, coarsely chopped
450 g (1 lb) old potatoes, peeled and diced
1 celery stick, diced
450 g (1 lb) leeks, diced
salt and freshly ground white pepper
1.2 litres (2 pints) chicken or vegetable stock
1 large bunch of fresh parsley
200 ml (7 fl oz) cream (optional)
1 bunch of fresh chives, snipped (optional)

*H*eat the oil and fry the onions or shallots for 1 minute without allowing them to colour. Add the potatoes and celery and fry for 1 minute. Season and add the whites of the leeks. Add the stock and parsley stalks, cover and simmer for about 30 minutes until the potatoes are soft. Allow to cool. Either liquidize all the ingredients for a thick soup, or pound with a potato masher for a chunkier presentation. To serve, heat through, add cream if desired, check the seasoning and add the freshly chopped leek greens, parsley and chives.

Variations

Cawl can be boosted as a vegetarian soup by adding some cooked, diced French or runner beans, some snipped sun-dried tomatoes, some diced avocado, or lots of fresh herbs, particularly basil or coriander.

For a gourmet traditional *Gower Oyster Soup*, add some shucked (de-shelled) oysters, sautéed quickly in a little butter, adding all the oyster juices. Other shellfish, such as mussels, scallops or queens can be served the same way.

A few flakes of smoked mackerel or haddock, or any cold, poached fish, can be added with the leeks for extra depth of flavour.

Cold cooked ham, lamb or chicken diced to 1 cm ($^1/_2$ in) pieces may also be added.

———————————— • ————————————

Green herb soup with cream cheese dressing

Similar to *Cawl Cennin*, but this takes in different vegetables and herbs for extra interest and flavour. When they are in season, this soup is particularly good with a range of green vegetables such as spinach or even seabeet or watercress. Using these, stunning green soups with herby depths can easily be made.

Serves 4-6
1 tablespoon oil
225 g (8 oz) onions, thinly sliced
225 g (8 oz) carrots, thinly sliced
100 g (4 oz) celery, thinly sliced
2 garlic cloves, thinly sliced
salt and freshly ground black pepper
$^1/_2$ teaspoon paprika
2 bunches of watercress, chopped
1 bunch of fresh parsley, chopped
650 ml (1$^1/_2$ pints) chicken or vegetable stock
100 g (4 oz) curd cheese
1 teaspoon pesto (basil) sauce
100 ml (4$^1/_2$ fl oz) cream

*H*eat the oil and fry the vegetables and garlic gently until soft but not coloured at all. Season with salt and pepper and add the paprika and watercress. Reserve a little parsley for garnish then add the remainder to the pan. Cover and cook for 1 minute until wilted. Add the stock, bring to the boil then simmer for 10 minutes. Cool slightly and liquidize to make a bright green soup. Return it to the pan.

Mix the curd cheese with the pesto then shape into ovals using two teaspoons. Heat through the soup and stir in the cream. Float the cheese on top and sprinkle with the reserved parsley to serve.

---

*P*UMPKIN OR MARROW SOUP

*T*his recipe uses a basic mashed pumpkin, just like the one on page 46, to make a delicious soup.

Serves 4
1 kg (2 lb) pumpkin or marrow
2 tablespoons oil
225 g (8 oz) mixed onion, carrot and celery, cut into 2 cm (¹/₂ in) dice
2 garlic cloves, crushed
1 teaspoon dried basil or tarragon
350 g (12 oz) tomatoes, chopped
salt and freshly ground black pepper
600 ml (1 pint) milk or chicken or vegetable stock
2 large sprigs of fresh parsley or coriander, chopped
4 slices bread fried into small croûtons

*P*re-heat the oven to 200ºC/400ºF/gas 6. Cut the pumpkin or marrow in half and bake in the pre-heated oven for 30 minutes or until soft. Scoop out and discard the seeds then cut the soft pulp away from the skin.

Heat the oil and fry the vegetables until beginning to colour. Add the pumpkin, garlic, basil and tomatoes. Season with salt and pepper. Add the milk or stock and simmer for 20 minutes, stirring frequently. Liquidize to form a smooth, thick soup. Re-heat, if necessary, then garnish with freshly chopped parsley or coriander and small, crispy croûtons.

LIGHT MEALS
AND SNACKS

HOME-MADE HOUMOUS WITH VARIATIONS

Houmous is hardly Welsh, but I was introduced to Middle Eastern cooking thirty years ago when my uncle married a Lebanese lady. I discovered many new flavours at their dinner parties. With the internationalization of cuisine in restaurants, ingredients such as houmous, chick peas, aubergines, harissa (hot pepper sauce) and tahini, to name just a few, are quite commonly used. Using a food processor, the job of making all sorts of blended dishes becomes simple. It's even simpler if you use tinned chick peas for houmous, but I like to boil my own with some aromats and spices to enhance their flavour, and their texture is far nuttier than the pressure-cooked tinned ones.

Nevertheless, chick peas are fairly bland whatever you do to them, so to introduce other flavours beyond the basic garlic and tahini can transform houmous. It is certainly very receptive to other flavours such as lemon, tomato, harissa, anchovy and olives, and you can experiment at very little cost with many others.

Serves 4
2 tablespoons oil
225 g (8 oz) onions, coarsely chopped
100 g (4 oz) carrots, coarsely chopped
4 garlic cloves, crushed
15 g (½ oz) root ginger, scraped and sliced
450 g (1 lb) chick peas
300 ml (10 fl oz) dry white wine or cider
1 chilli pepper
1 large sprig of fresh marjoram or thyme
salt and freshly ground black pepper
2-3 tablespoons olive oil
2-3 tablespoons tahini

Heat the oil and fry the onions and carrots for 1 minute. Add the garlic, ginger and chick peas and cook for 2-3 minutes. Add the wine or cider, chilli pepper and herbs, cover and allow the flavours to absorb for a few minutes.

Cover with water, season with salt and pepper and simmer briskly for 1 hour, topping up with water as necessary, until the peas are softish. Allow to cool then remove the chilli and woody herbs and husks.

Process the peas in a food processor, adding a little water and oil as necessary to form a thick paste. Blend in the tahini. Adjust the seasoning to taste.
Serve with crudités (raw vegetables cut in batons), hot pitta bread, ciabatta, focaccia or French baguette with olives, gherkins, capers and cocktail onions.

Variations
Split the houmous into four parts: leave one plain; add six sun-dried tomatoes to another; 1 tablespoon of pesto sauce to a third; the juice and grated zest of a lemon to the fourth.

Other variations can include adding: 6 pitted green olives; 6 pitted black olives; a large bunch of chopped fresh coriander; 6 crushed garlic cloves; 3 chopped pickled chillies; 3 chopped anchovy fillets.

QUICK VEGETARIAN PIE

*T*his is a quick cottage pie I slapped together one day, but which was very well received by the two young ladies for whom I cooked it. The curd cheese helps the flavours of the vegetables come together under a potato crust. You can combine any vegetables, and a touch of fresh herbs and a hint of spice can transform blander flavours.

Serves 4
450 g (1 lb) cooked vegetables such as carrots, celery, broccoli, peas,
sweetcorn, spinach, cabbage
½ teaspoon freshly grated nutmeg
100 g (4 oz) low-fat curd cheese
2 spring onions, finely chopped
350 g (12 oz) mashed potato
50 g (2 oz) butter
1-3 tablespoons milk (optional)

*P*re-heat the oven to 200°C/400°F/gas 6. Cut the cooked vegetables into even-sized pieces and put in a pie dish. Sprinkle with a few drops of water and the nutmeg. Mix the curd cheese with the spring onions then fork them over the vegetables. Mix the mashed potato with the butter and a little milk if necessary, then fork over the top to form a seal on the pie. Mark a swirling pattern over the potato and bake in the pre-heated oven for 20 minutes until heated through and golden brown on top.

GRATIN OF LEEKS, ROOT VEGETABLES AND CHEESE SAUCE

This is a wonderful homely dish with great flavour. You can vary the vegetables and the cheese to suit your own taste.

Serves 4
450 g (1 lb) young leeks
100 g (4 oz) baby turnips
100 g (4 oz) baby carrots
½ teaspoon chopped fresh basil
3 tablespoons oil
salt and freshly ground black pepper
100 g (4 oz) Cheddar cheese, grated
1 egg
1 teaspoon mustard
150 ml (5 fl oz) glass dry sherry or cider
225 g (8 oz) onions, thinly sliced

Pre-heat the oven to 200ºC/400ºF/gas 6. Trim and cut the leeks into quarters, lengthways, to 2.5 cm (1 in) from the base. Rinse in cold water to remove any earth. Shake dry and cut into 7.5 cm (3 in) lengths, using all the leek. Trim and cut the turnips and carrots into 7.5 cm (3 in) thin strips. Mix them with the leeks, basil and a little oil and salt and pepper. Either heat a little oil and stir-fry the vegetables quickly, or arrange them neatly in a gratin dish, all facing one way, cover and microwave for 1-2 minutes until just soft. If you have fried them, arrange them neatly in a gratin dish.

Mix together the cheese, egg, mustard, sherry or cider and salt and pepper. Spread evenly over the leeks and bake in the pre-heated oven for 5-7 minutes until golden and sizzling.

Meanwhile, heat the remaining oil and fry the onions until very golden and crisp. Serve on the cheese topping for extra crunch.

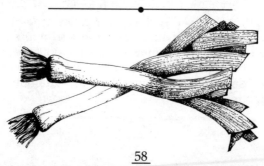

LEEKS

GRATIN OF SEAFOOD WITH LAVERBREAD

You can cook this in a large gratin dish, or make it in individual gratin dishes. The dish can be varied using any combination of seafoods such as shellfish – cockles and mussels; cooked or tinned fish – salmon or tuna; smoked fish – flaked mackerel, kippers, haddock, whiting or cod. It is also delicious using cold, diced meat, particularly ham or lamb, in place of fish. It can even be adapted as a vegetarian dish using any cooked vegetables – courgettes, carrots, beans, peas, cabbage, potatoes. The irony flavour of the seaweed and the crunchy, herby topping give a good contrast of flavours and textures. You can use any combination of herbs for the crumb topping.

Serves 4
225 g (8 oz) fresh cod, or hake, or monkfish (or any fresh white fish), skinned and boned
100 g (4 oz) shelled prawns (defrosted naturally)
100 g (4 oz) scallops, sliced 1 cm (½ in) thick
juice ½ lemon
dash of tabasco sauce
225 g (8 oz) laverbread
4 slices stale brown bread
½ teaspoon dried herbs de provence (or fresh herbs – parsley, basil, oregano)
1 garlic clove (optional)
50 g (2 oz) butter or margarine, chilled and diced
freshly ground black pepper

Pre-heat the oven to 200ºC/400ºF/gas 6. First cut the fish into 1 cm (½ in) slices. Put in a bowl and mix in the prawns and scallops. Add the lemon juice and tabasco, mix and leave for a few moments. Spoon the laverbread into a gratin dish, or divide between individual dishes.

Make breadcrumbs from the stale brown bread in a food processor. Add the herbs and garlic (optional) and very cold butter, cut in small pieces, to form a crumbly mixture.

Cover the laverbread with the fish and juice, distributing evenly and pressing slightly into the soft laverbread. Sprinkle the breadcrumb mixture over to cover completely but do not compress it into the fish. Add a sprinkling of pepper. Put the dish(es) into the pre-heated oven for about 5-7 minutes until the fish is just cooked and the top is crisp and golden. Serve immediately.

SAUTÉED MACKEREL FILLETS WITH ONIONS

*T*his is best made with mackerel that is as fresh as possible, or whole fresh
sardines are very good cooked in this way.

Serves 8 as a starter or 4 as a main course
8 x 225 g (8 oz) mackerel
1 tablespoon plain flour
1 teaspoon paprika
2 tablespoons olive oil
225 g (8 oz) onions or shallots, thinly sliced
50 g (2 oz) butter
1 lemon, cut into wedges
1 tablespoon chopped fresh parsley

*F*illet the mackerel, removing any small bones and fins. Do not wash the fish,
just pat it dry with kitchen paper. Mix the flour and paprika and dust over the
fish. Heat the oil and fry the onions quickly until just turning golden, then
reserve or push them to the side of the pan. Melt the butter in the onion oil,
then fry the fish, skin uppermost, for 30 seconds. Turn over to cook skin-side
down for barely a minute, topping with onions during cooking. Serve
immediately with lemon wedges and chopped parsley.

———————•———————

SMOKED FISH AND LEEK KEDGEREE

*I*t's good to see kedgeree popular once again as all ingredients, except the rice of
course, can be found on the Welsh coast. There are leeks from Gower, smoked
cod from Swansea docks, Milford or specialists such as Welsh Smoked Products
– and there are good cooks, too, such as Patrick at Patrick's Restaurant in
Mumbles. His version uses brown rice, which has a good, nutty flavour. It
takes twice as long to cook but is worthwhile as the wholewheat gives extra
flavour.

Serves 4-6
750 g (1½ lb) smoked cod or haddock
225 g (8 oz) onions, sliced
100 g (4 oz) carrots, thinly sliced
1 celery stick, sliced
2 tablespoons oil
50 g (2 oz) butter

225 g (8 oz) brown rice
50 g (2 oz) wheat
1/2 teaspoon paprika
150 ml (5 fl oz) dry white wine
600 ml (1 pint) of stock (see method below)
6 hard-boiled eggs
50 ml (2 fl oz) dry sherry
2 large sprigs fresh parsley, roughly chopped

FOR THE SAUCE
225 g (8 oz) onions, finely chopped
1 tablespoon oil
25 g (1 oz) butter
1 teaspoon mild curry paste or curry powder
150 ml (5 fl oz) water or stock
150 ml (5 fl oz) tomato juice
50 ml (2 fl oz) cream

If the fish has its skin, cut into slices about 2 cm (1 in) thick, pull away from the skin, and remove any bones. Use the skin to make a stock, boiling it with the trimmings from the onion, carrot and celery. Otherwise make up about 600 ml (1 pint) of stock, using fish, chicken or vegetable stock cubes.

In a large pan, fry the onions, carrots and celery in a little oil until soft but not brown. Add the butter then the rice, wheat and paprika, frying together for 2-3 minutes. Add the wine, mixing well, then stir in 300 ml (10 fl oz) of stock, cover and simmer for 15 minutes, stirring occasionally. Add the fish, distributing it evenly and pressing it into the rice. Add more stock as necessary, and continue to cook for 10-15 minutes, covered, without stirring, topping up with stock to keep moist. When the rice is just soft but not soggy, arrange the eggs on top, pressing in slightly. Sprinkle with sherry, top with parsley, and cover and leave for a minute.

Meanwhile, make the sauce by frying the onions in the oil and butter for 5 minutes until soft and just slightly golden. Add the curry paste (if using powder, add when onions are half cooked and stir well), the water or stock, and cook for 5 minutes. Then add the tomato juice and heat through, mixing well. Finish with the cream to form a smooth sauce. Serve with the kedgeree.

————————————•————————————

CARMARTHEN HAM

The old farmhouse sustenance throughout the winter came from cured ham and bacon from the farmyard porker. Hams were cured in the large chimneys of farm kitchens, which slowly dried the salted ham and bacon. This tradition has largely died out in Wales, yet the remaining few producers make products that are not dissimilar to Bayonne, Serrano or Parma hams from the Continent. In Carmarthen market, Albert Rees's shop still sells these traditional hams. The freshly cured ones are sliced for grilling. Slightly older, they are ideal for boiling as a York ham. Those cured for many months are sliced wafer thin like Parma ham, and have a similar farmyard flavour that is utterly delicious. The hocks have a great flavour, but need to be boiled for ages to soften the meat: they make a great base for a winter stew, or even a summer 'paysanne' salad.

———————————●———————————

COUNTRY HAM WITH VEGETABLE STEW

The flavour of lovage, which is far too overpowering for most dishes, actually enhances boiled ham, giving an amazing depth to the flavour. Croûtons spread with anchovy sauce make a good contrasting accompaniment. For a tasty variation use yellow split peas instead of puy lentils, which will break up and make a very thick sauce or soup that your spoon will stand up in – chunky and delicious.

Serves 4
1 hock of ham, about 900 g (2 lb)
225 g (8 oz) puy lentils
225 g (8 oz) onions, cut into 2 cm (½ in) dice
225 g (8 oz) carrots, cut into 2 cm (½ in) dice
225 g (8 oz) parsnips, turnips or swede, cut into 2 cm (½ in) dice
225 g (8 oz) celery, cut into 2 cm (½ in) dice
1 large sprig of fresh lovage (optional)
1 sprig of fresh thyme, roughly chopped or ½ teaspoon dried thyme
6 bay leaves
12 black peppercorns, crushed
1 large bunch of fresh parsley, chopped
1 tablespoon wine vinegar

Place the ham in the pan and cover with water. Bring to the boil then simmer briskly for 10 minutes. Test the water for saltiness. If it is excessive, discard the water and repeat, simmering for about 30 minutes and topping up with water as necessary. Add the lentils and vegetables and return to the simmer. Add the lovage, thyme, bay leaves and crushed peppercorns, partially cover and simmer for 45-60 minutes until all the vegetables and lentils are soft and the meat can be eased off the bone.

Remove the bay leaves, thyme twigs and ham. Push the meat from the bones, discard any skin, fat and gristle, roughly chop the meat and return it to the stew. Add the parsley and vinegar and serve piping hot as a great winter warmer.

MUSSELS WITH SMOKED CAERPHILLY

The Queen's Head, Glanwydden, in the Conwy Valley, uses the renowned Conwy mussels for this award-winning dish. You can often buy cooked, fresh mussels in the markets. Most frozen packaged mussel meats are horrible and have a powdery texture. If you have excess mussels from a freshly made dish, de-shell and put them in a container covered with mussel juice and freeze. They will keep in good condition for 6-8 weeks. The mild smokey flavour of smoked Caerphilly goes well with seafoods, so you can use any shellfish for this dish: cockles, prawns, queen scallops, or any white fish, even cold poached leftovers, or a tin of tuna fish.

Serves 4
25 g (1 oz) butter
1 garlic clove, finely chopped
1 tablespoon chopped fresh parsley
350 g (12 oz) mussel meats
freshly ground black pepper
50 g (2 oz) smoked Caerphilly, grated
wholemeal bread to serve

Pre-heat the grill. Melt the butter and fry the garlic and parsley for about 30 seconds. Add the mussels and heat through for just 1 minute, then season with pepper. Put into individual flameproof serving dishes, top with cheese and grill for a minute until golden. Serve immediately with wholemeal bread. A green or tomato salad goes well with this rich dish.

PANCAKES STUFFED WITH CARMARTHEN HAM AND WILD MUSHROOMS WITH A SAVOURY CUSTARD

*P*ancakes make good light meals, and are especially popular on the Continent, where crêperies offer dozens of combinations of fillings. Pancakes are easy to make and fillings can be crafted or whisked up from leftovers. For successful pancakes you need to make the mix a little in advance, and have a good pan that will not stick. You can buy pancake pans which are like a very shallow frying pan, and are a worthwhile investment. You can add finely chopped fresh herbs to the batter to give an extra flavour, or some finely chopped cooked spinach, or even a tablespoon of laverbread for a seafood flavour.

Makes 8 pancakes
FOR THE PANCAKES
1 egg
50 g (2 oz) plain or buckwheat flour
150 ml (5 fl oz) milk
1 tablespoon butter, melted
pinch of salt

FOR THE FILLING
2 teaspoons oil
100 g (4 oz) onions or shallots, finely chopped
225 g (8 oz) wild mushrooms, ceps, girolles, morels
or button mushrooms, all thinly sliced
1 garlic clove, crushed (optional)
2 sprigs of fresh parsley, finely chopped
100 g (4 oz) Carmarthen ham or Bayonne, Serrano or sliced cooked ham, cut into 2 cm
(1 in) pieces
25 ml (1 fl oz) dry Madeira or sherry
50 ml (2 fl oz) cream
1 teaspoon mild mustard
salt and freshly ground black pepper

FOR THE SAVOURY CUSTARD
1 egg
150 ml (5 fl oz) cream
1 teaspoon mustard
dash of paprika
pinch of salt
grated cheese (optional)

freshly chopped parsley (optional)
1 teaspoon olive paste, sun-dried tomato paste, tomato purée, pesto sauce
or coriander sauce (optional)

To make the pancakes, beat the egg well then add the flour and milk to form a smooth, flowing creamy mixture, adding the butter and salt. Leave for 30 minutes to develop the texture, but always whisk again before use.

Lightly oil and heat a pancake pan – I use a 20 cm (8 in) frying pan – until just lightly smoking. Use a ladle to judge the correct amount of mix required. Pour into the pan and immediately tilt so the entire surface is covered with the thinnest possible veneer. Cook for about 20-30 seconds then turn using a palette knife or a quick flick of the wrist! If the pancakes are to be filled you can just cook them on one side, ensuring the surface is completely dry before removing from the pan, but I always like both sides cooked. Put a 5 cm (2 in) square of butter paper in the centre between each to stop them sticking together. They can be made in advance, but are best used fresh if possible.

To make the filling, heat the oil and fry the onions or shallots until soft. Add the mushrooms and garlic, if using, and cook for 2-3 minutes until softened and just colouring. Add the parsley, ham and Madeira or sherry, heating through quickly. Mix in the cream and mustard, season and heat to thicken.

To make the sauce, mix together all the main ingredients, beating well until smooth. For extra richness, you can stir in grated cheese or herbs, or the paste, purée or sauce of your choice.

Spread spoonfuls of the filling mixture on one half of each pancake, then roll them up and arrange in a shallow flameproof dish. Cover the pancakes with the sauce, if using, then put under a medium grill or in a warm oven until heated through and the sauce is golden on top.

Filling Variations
Substitute any white fish for the ham and mushrooms, adding some crabmeat, fresh prawns, cockles, mussels, even oysters for a good seafood crêpe.

Some hot *Quick Ratatouille* (see page 145) makes a perfect vegetarian filling.

Fillings can be added cold, then heated through in the oven with the sauce. Try: smoked salmon or sewin, curd cheese and avocado, sun-dried tomatoes, spinach and Ricotta cheese, tuna fish and chopped tomatoes.

SALAD PAYSANNE WITH CARMARTHEN HAM AND LENTILS

This is the summer recipe for using a hock of ham, serving a warm salad as a
light meal or starter.

Serves 4
1 hock of Carmarthen ham, cooked with vegetables and lentils (see Country Ham
with Vegetable Stew *page 62)*
25 ml (1 fl oz) red wine or balsamic vinegar
4 tablespoons olive oil
1 garlic clove, crushed
4 slices stale wholemeal bread, diced
1 large bowl of mixed salad leaves
1 bunch of fresh parsley, finely chopped
1 teaspoon mustard
1 teaspoon pesto sauce
50 ml (2 fl oz) water

When the ham is cooked, remove meat and bay leaves, stalks and peel from
the stock, and boil this down until it just covers the lentils and vegetables. Pour
it into a bowl, add half the red wine or balsamic vinegar, cool and refrigerate
overnight to form a jelly. Meanwhile, cut meat from the bone, discarding the fat
and skin, and chop into 1 cm (1/2 in) cubes.

To assemble the salad, first make some crispy bread garlic croûtons. Heat the
oil and fry the crushed garlic for a few seconds, then add the bread cubes and
fry until just crisp. Remove and add the meat cubes and heat through quickly.

Put the salad into a large bowl and dredge with parsley and half the olive oil,
mixing gently to coat all the leaves. Arrange on large plates with four
teaspoons of the jellied lentils and vegetables. Top leaves with croûtons and
ham. Put the mustard, pesto, remaining oil, vinegar and water into a jar, shake
vigorously and pour on to the edges of the salads and serve.

PASTA WITH RUNNER BEANS AND BACON

A great summer supper at home was always freshly cooked runner beans
with a generous knob of Welsh salted butter and a few rashers of smoked
bacon. The pasta combines perfectly with this dish to make a healthy,
nutritional meal.

Serves 4
450 g (1 lb) fresh, young runner beans, trimmed and thinly sliced
225 g (8 oz) fresh pasta, either penne or fusilli
salt and freshly ground black pepper
2 tablespoons extra virgin olive oil
100 g (4 oz) smoked streaky bacon, rinded
1 small bunch of fresh marjoram, finely chopped, or a pinch of dried marjoram
50 g (2 oz) Parmesan, Pecorino or Cheddar, freshly slivered (optional)

*F*irst fill two pans with hot, salted water, one for the pasta and one for the
beans. Both cook best in a generous amount of hot, well salted water. Cook the
beans at a brisk simmer in one and the pasta in the other, stirring the pasta
occasionally until *al dente*, with firmness and maximum flavour. Drain and
season both with salt and pepper, drizzling with olive oil. Keep them warm.

Meanwhile, cook the bacon in a hot pan until just browning at the edges and
all the fat is sizzling. Put on to a board and slice into pieces the size of the
pasta. In a large bowl, mix the beans, pasta and bacon carefully with the bacon
juice and herbs, and sprinkle with Parmesan, Pecorino or Cheddar, if using, for
extra flavour. Serve immediately.

———————————●———————————

HERBY TOAD IN THE HOLE

Now that almost every butcher and supermarket sells good sausages, this dish should become a popular high tea or supper snack once again. By adding the extra dimension of onions and other vegetables, the flavours are more complex and sustaining. These are also a good base for a gravy, which can be made with beer to go with beef sausages, or cider if using pork. The same formulae can apply to the batter!

Serves 4
450 g (1 lb) good quality sausages of your choice
225 g (8 oz) onions, thinly sliced
100 g (4 oz) carrots, thinly sliced
100 g (4 oz) celery, thinly sliced
2 teaspoons oil
2 teaspoons roughly chopped fresh mixed herbs or 1 teaspoon dried herbs
½ teaspoon barbecue spice
salt and freshly ground black pepper

FOR THE BATTER
2 eggs, beaten
100 g (4 oz) plain flour
300 ml (10 fl oz) beer or cider
pinch of salt

FOR THE GRAVY
300 ml (10 fl oz) beer or cider
2 teaspoons gravy granules
2 teaspoons English mustard powder, diluted
with 100 ml (3 fl oz) water or beer

Pre-heat the oven to 200ºC/400ºF/gas 6. Put the sausages and vegetables in the roasting tray, lightly oiling them all, then bake in the pre-heated oven for 15 minutes, turning several times so the sausages brown evenly and the vegetables colour to golden. Cook for longer if the sausages are thick. Sprinkle with herbs, spice and black pepper and cook a further 5 minutes or until the sausages are just cooked.

Meanwhile, make the batter by combining the ingredients in a bowl, mixing well. Leave to stand for at least 15 minutes.

Transfer any excess oil off the sausages and vegetables to a pan, and add about a quarter of the cooked vegetables. Arrange the cooked sausages neatly in the roasting tray and pour over the batter, which should just cover everything. Return to the oven for a further 10-15 minutes or until the 'pudding' has risen and is golden on top.

Meanwhile, add the beer or cider to the pan and boil for a few minutes. Sprinkle in the gravy granules, then add the diluted mustard and simmer for a few minutes. Check and adjust the seasoning. Serve the pudding with the onion and mustard gravy.

---

*F*LAT MUSHROOMS WITH BACON AND GORGONZOLA

*T*his tasty, quick snack comes from Patrick's Restaurant in Mumbles.

Serves 4
25 g (1 oz) butter
225 g (8 oz) large, flat mushrooms, stalks removed
½ red pepper, cut into 8 thin strips
100 g (4 oz) smoked streaky bacon, rinded and cut into 2.5 cm (1 in) pieces
100 g (4 oz) Gorgonzola
2 large sprigs of fresh parsley

*P*re-heat the oven to 200°C / 400°F / gas 6 or pre-heat the grill to full. Melt a little butter and fry the mushroom caps for a minute on either side until just lightly browning. Put into individual warmed serving bowls and keep warm. Fry the pepper slices until beginning to soften, then add the bacon and cook until the fat is just turning light golden. Put into the mushroom caps, top each with a slice of Gorgonzola and put into the pre-heated oven or under the grill until sizzling. Top generously with parsley and serve with a green salad.

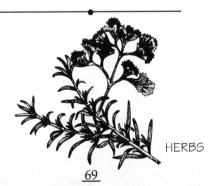

HERBS

69

WILD MUSHROOM AND SCALLOP CROUSTADE

An award-winning dish from the Crown at Whitebrook, the texture of seared
scallops is remarkably similar to good wild mushrooms, particularly the
'penny bun' or cep. The crispy case gives the crunch to the dish.

Serves 4
FOR THE CROUSTADE CASES
100 g (4 oz) breadcrumbs
100 g (4 oz) ground hazelnuts
100 g (4 oz) pine nuts, chopped
½ teaspoon dried mixed herbs
50 g (2 oz) butter, diced
salt and freshly ground black pepper

FOR THE FILLING
50 g (2 oz) butter or oil
4 fresh scallops (optional but good)
50 g (2 oz) shallots, finely chopped
450 g (1 lb) wild mushrooms, sliced
150 ml (5 fl oz) cream
2 teaspoons chopped fresh parsley
50 ml (2 fl oz) walnut oil
1 teaspoon sherry vinegar
1 bowl of mixed salad leaves

Pre-heat the oven to 180ºC/350ºF/gas 4. Rub together the breadcrumbs, nuts,
herbs and butter to form a crumble. Season with salt and pepper. Press into
pastry cases to form neat cups. Bake in the pre-heated oven for 10-15 minutes
until just crisp and set.

Meanwhile, melt a little butter or oil and fry the scallops quickly on both sides
in a very hot pan until golden. Remove and keep warm. Add the shallots to the
pan and fry for 1 minute until just turning golden, then add the mushrooms
and stir-fry quickly to soften. Add the cream and heat through for 2-3 minutes,
stirring so that the flavours blend.

Fill the cases with the mushrooms and sauce. Slice the scallops and top the
cases with these, drenching with a little parsley. Mix together the walnut oil
and vinegar and use to dress the salad. Serve with the croustade.

WELSH RAREBIT

*T*his tasty cheese dish is far more than just cheese melted on toast. It is a combination of condiments that can be quite mild or fairly racey. I find this basic mixture successful every time and I vary it to make it as exotic as the occasion or mood demands. You can add sherry instead of beer, or even port, Madeira or wine. Try it with different cheese, even combinations of soft and hard cheeses, cutting them all into small pieces before adding them to the mixture. Combinations of herbs – parsley, thyme, marjoram, coriander – bring a multitude of flavour variations. Different spices – nutmeg, allspice, cloves or curry powder – give an extra zip. The toast can be coated with Marmite or Bovril, a thin spread of laverbread, or sun-dried tomato paste before topping with the rarebit mixture.
Some lightly cooked diced fruit – such as diced apple fried in butter like they serve at Dolmelynllyn Hall – gives a good contrast, or some finely diced blanched leek or onion adds an extra savoury nuance.
Welsh rarebit can also be used to crown vegetables, fish or just baked beans!

Serves 4
175 g (6 oz) Welsh Cheddar, grated
½ teaspoon dry English mustard
75 ml (3 fl oz) bitter beer or cider
½ teaspoon Worcestershire sauce
few twists of freshly ground black pepper
dash of cayenne pepper
1 egg
4 slices toast, buttered

*M*ix together the main ingredients then spread over the toast. Place on a grill rack and grill for 3-5 minutes until golden on top.

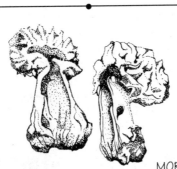

MOREL MUSHROOMS

MAIN COURSES - FISH

BASS

Bass is the most beautiful sea fish, even called salmon bass in many areas, as it has a silver belly which darkens to pale blue grey on its sides, deepening to charcoal blue black on the back. It is a great sporting fish, and thrives in rough weather. On spring tides on Gower, they are caught in the rock gullies of the headlands as they search for crabs and other food in the chafing shallows. Bill Hill at Hen Dafarn cooked bass he'd netted that day. He always scales and guts the fish on the shore as we do on Gower. It saves a mess in the kitchen, and the scales slide off easily when the fish is fresh from the water. If they dry out it is very hard work. Just rub the fish from tail to head with the flat of a knife and the scales slither off.

SEA BASS WITH BEURRE BLANC

This is a beautiful way to cook bass. You can serve it straight from the oven with its own juices, or you can make a *beurre blanc* sauce to accompany the fish. This legendary sauce was invented, reputedly by accident, at Château Goulaine in the Muscadet area of the Loire Valley. All restaurants in this area now serve a variation of this sauce, and when I first tried it in 1975 at Château Cassemichère, I spent the next two weeks sampling fish with *beurre blanc* to discover the secrets of this amazing flavour. Now every chef in Britain has a version, but either the flavour of the sauce tends to be too light or too much cream is added, which spoils it. This is the version I developed and served in my restaurants every day for fifteen years. You can also serve it with any baked, poached or grilled fish, vegetables and even light meats.

Serves 4
2 x 600 g (1¼ lb) sea bass, cleaned and scaled
1 large bunch of fresh herbs such as parsley, marjoram, sage, fennel, thyme
225 g (8 oz) leeks, roughly chopped
salt and freshly ground black pepper
½ lemon, sliced
150 ml (5 fl oz) dry white wine
25 g (1 oz) butter

FOR THE BEURRE BLANC
100 g (4 oz) shallots, finely chopped
12 white peppercorns, crushed
300 ml (10 fl oz) Muscadet
1 tablespoon white wine vinegar
225 g (8 oz) very lightly salted butter (or use unsalted and one or two blobs
salted to taste), cut into 8 pieces
small dash of cayenne
juice ½ lemon

Pre-heat the oven to 200ºC/400ºF/gas 6. Fill the cavity of the bass with herbs. Put the leeks into a roasting tray and place the fish on top. Season with salt and pepper and cover with some lemon slices. Pour over the wine and dot with butter. Bake in the pre-heated oven for 20-30 minutes, testing with a skewer to ensure it is just cooked through. It will slide from the tray on to a warmed serving platter. Cover loosely with foil to keep warm if necessary. The butter and juices combine to make a good light sauce.

To make the *beurre blanc*, it is essential to use an enamel pan, as even a good quality stainless steel pan gives a slightly metallic taste to the sauce. Put the shallots, peppercorns, wine and wine vinegar in a 15 cm (6 in) pan and simmer very gently for at least 30 minutes for the flavours to mingle slowly into one another and for the juice to evaporate to about a quarter. Tip into a bowl then strain the juice back into the pan, pressing down well to extract all the juice. (Put the shallots into the stockpot or fish soup, as they still contain much flavour.) Allow the juice to boil down until about 5 mm (¼ in) covers the pan. Over a low to medium heat and using a small balloon whisk, beat in the first piece of butter. Once it has been absorbed, add the next, and continue piece by piece until it has all emulsified into a creamy sauce that looks like a light mayonnaise. Add a dash of cayenne and lemon juice, mixing well. Cover and keep warm, but do not overheat as it will separate. If keeping a while, give an occasional whisk to keep it smooth. Serve in a sauce boat.

Variations
Beurre blanc will not re-heat once cooled, but can be used to make garlic and herb butter that will have the most superb flavour. The flavour of *beurre blanc* can be varied by adding freshly chopped herbs as appropriate: chervil for fish or asparagus; tarragon for chicken; basil or coriander for fish and shellfish; sorrel or chives for salmon or sewin; mint for new season's Welsh lamb.

GOWER LOBSTER WITH BEURRE BLANC

𝒯he Bristol channel has one of the highest tidal ranges in the world. On a spring tide at the equinox, the rise is 12 or more metres (45 feet). Hence, vast expanses of rocks and sand are exposed at low tide. The extreme low rocky area is the habitat of many lobsters and crabs. The layered limestone rock of Gower provides many holes and ledges where these creatures naturally hide, and certain pools contain famous 'lobster holes' where, over the generations, numerous creatures have been caught by those who know these secret pools. Many of these are named, just as the famous salmon pools on rivers are named. At Rhossili on a very drab, windy day we were able to fish the 'Top Ledge', 'Bottom Ledge', and 'Waterfall Hole', alas without success, but did winkle out a fine 675 g (1½ lb) lobster from the 'Window Hole', which I cooked at Fairyhill with Paul Davies.

A cock lobster is best used for salads as it has large claws containing succulent meat. A hen lobster is preferable for dishes with sauces as the roe inside gives an exceptional depth to the flavour of the sauce. The tail of the hen is broader than that of the cock, and the top swimmerettes are soft compared to the male's hard bony ones.

Serves 2
1 x 675 g (1½ lb) lobster (preferably a hen)
225 g (8 oz) mixed onions, carrots and celery, chopped
1 sprig of fresh thyme
3 bay leaves
½ teaspoon cayenne
6 black peppercorns, crushed
about 100 g (4 oz) salt, to taste
50 g (2 oz) butter

FOR THE SAUCE
1 tablespoon butter
1 tablespoon oil
½ red pepper, cut into 2.5 cm (1 in) thin strips
50 g (2 oz) shallots, sliced
100 g (4 oz) small leek, cut into 2.5 cm (1 in) strips
75 ml (3 fl oz) good dry white wine such as Muscadet or Chablis
120 ml (4 fl oz) beurre blanc (see page 73)
1 teaspoon tomato purée (optional)
1 teaspoon chopped fresh parsley or coriander

$\mathcal{T}$o cook the lobster you need a large pan with a lid and enough boiling water to immerse the lobster completely. The water should be as salty as the sea, but I underdo the salt so the water can then be used for soup or stock. Boil the water with all the other ingredients for 5 minutes, then hold the lobster firmly over the back, tucking the tail underneath, and drop it, tail first, into the water and put on the lid. Return to a simmer and cook for 1 minute, then remove from the pan and cool.

If you are eating the lobster plain, hot or cold, cook for 3 minutes per 450 g (1 lb) then allow to cool in the water until warm or cold, as required. It will absorb the flavours of the herbs and aromats. You can store the lobster in the water in the fridge for 2-3 days.

Put the lobster on a board with the tail extended and split lengthways using a heavy knife. Discard the stomach sac from the head and the viscera from the tail. Reserve any juices from inside. Do not rinse it under water as many misguided chefs do, as this will wash away the flavour. Scrape out all gungy meat from the head or carapace. If you have a hen (female) lobster, it will have a red to black mixture - the eggs - which should be mixed with its liver for a really good sauce. A cock (male) will only have the pale greeny liver. Whichever you have, mash either the eggs and liver, or just the liver, very well with 25 g (1 oz) butter and reserve.

Disjoint the claws and carefully crack the end joint, removing the meat in the largest possible pieces and discarding the sinews. Use a small knife or pick to extract meat from other joints. Cut the tail meat into four or five pieces, and keep the shell just warm (even in the bouillon).

To make the sauce, heat the oil and butter and fry the pepper and shallots until softening. Add the leek and cook together, pouring in the wine and any juices from the lobster shell. When just soft, add the lobster meat and the flavoured butter, swirling the pan to mix well. The greeny butter made from the hen will turn bright orange, exactly as the lobster shell changes colour during cooking. Immediately add the *beurre blanc*, heating through gently as you swirl the pan for no longer than a minute. If you have a cock lobster you can add a teaspoon of tomato purée to the butter to give a brighter colour!

Put the shells on to warmed plates, fill with lobster pieces and vegetables with some sauce, spooning the rest on to the plate. Top with parsley and serve immediately.

BAKED COD WITH CREAMED VEGETABLES

*T*his dish from west Wales uses farm cream, root vegetables and the freshest fish in a dish that takes seconds to finalize, as most of it can be easily prepared in advance – another triumph from chef-patron Taffy at the Hollyland, Pembroke.

Serves 4
4 x 175 g (6 oz) cod fillets, skinned and boned
2 teaspoons oil
salt and freshly ground black pepper
100 g (4 oz) butter
175 g (6 oz) carrots, cut into julienne strips
175 g (6 oz) celery, cut into julienne strips
175 g (6 oz) onions, cut into julienne strips
175 g (6 oz) leeks, cut into julienne strips
300 ml (10 fl oz) whipping cream
pinch of freshly grated nutmeg
1 tablespoon chopped fresh parsley

*L*ightly oil and season the cod pieces. Melt the butter and gently fry the vegetables in a covered pan for about 5 minutes until just softening. Season with salt and pepper and stir in the cream. Simmer for a few minutes to thicken. Add the nutmeg and a little parsley and leave to cool. This can be stored in the fridge for later use, if desired.

Pre-heat the grill to medium. Use a large grill tray and spread four areas with vegetables slightly larger than the fish pieces. Top with the cod and put under the grill for about 5 minutes, until the cod is just cooked and the creamy vegetable mixture around the fish is turning golden. Use a fish slice to transfer the fish and vegetables to warmed plates, including all the crispy bits. Top with the remaining parsley and serve with mashed or boiled potatoes.

———————————●———————————

TROUT AND BACON

Wild brown trout from the turbulent Welsh streams have a very fine, clean flavour, unlike the muddy-tasting fish from sluggish brooks. A trout caught in early morning is part of a traditional breakfast or lunch, cooked with good Welsh bacon. We used to fish the Gower streams at Cheriton or Bishopston before leaving for school, and in the spring frequently returned with a brace or two of half-pounders, which were utterly delicious. You can now buy farmed trout everywhere. Many people are put off by the bones, but trout fillets are now readily available and very simple and quick to cook.

Serves 4
2 teaspoons oil
salt and freshly ground black pepper
4 x 175 g (6 oz) trout fillets
100 g (4 oz) shallots or onions, chopped
100 g (4 oz) smoked streaky bacon, rinded and chopped
2 teaspoons chopped or baby capers
120 ml (4 fl oz) dry wine or cider
1 tablespoon finely chopped fresh parsley

Lightly oil and season the fillets. Heat a little oil and fry the shallots or onions until soft, then push to the side of the pan. Add the bacon and fry until beginning to crispen, then push to the side. Place the fish flesh-side down in the pan and cook for 1 minute, then turn it over and pile the shallots and bacon on the top, adding the capers. Cover and cook for 2 minutes maximum just to crispen the skin. Lift out carefully with a fish slice and arrange on warmed serving plates. Add the wine or cider to the pan and boil quickly, adding the parsley and scraping up the juices from the pan. Pour over the fish and serve at once.

WELSH SEAFOOD COUSCOUS

Almost every country has a traditional fish casserole speciality, which no doubt originated from the fishermen's wives making a wholesome meal from the fish originally too small to send to the market. *Bouillabaisse* in France, *zarzuela* in Spain, and *brodetto* in Italy are internationally renowned. An abundance of local fish can be used in numerous variations on these themes. This is definitely a slosh-up dish and can be made from any fish. The base sauce derives the strong flavour from the crisp prawn shells, and other things can be dropped in, as when liquidized and sieved all the ugly trimmings disappear! Red mullet is particularly good, its liver and bones giving a good strong flavour.

Serves 4-6
*900 g (2 lb) mixed fish such as red mullet, grey mullet,
monkfish, cod, pin hake*
225 g (8 oz) cooked prawns in their shells
4 tablespoons olive oil
4 garlic cloves, crushed
450 g (1 lb) onions, roughly chopped
225 g (8 oz) carrots, roughly chopped
2 celery sticks, roughly chopped
1 red pepper, sliced
1 green pepper, sliced
1 teaspoon paprika
1 teaspoon ground coriander
450 ml (15 fl oz) dry white wine
225 g (8 oz) tomatoes, roughly chopped
1.2 litres (2 pints) water
1 sprig of fresh thyme
½ orange, squeezed
salt and freshly ground black pepper
450 g (1 lb) couscous
50 g (2 oz) butter
4 red chilli peppers
1 small bunch of fresh coriander, chopped

De-scale and fillet the fish, reserving the heads, livers and bones. Shell the prawns, reserving the meats and shells separately. Heat half the oil and fry the prawn shells for 10 minutes, stirring frequently until they turn very golden. Add the garlic, stirring in well for 2 minutes. Add half the vegetables and peppers, mixing well. Cover and cook over a medium heat for 3-4 minutes for all flavours to mingle. Add the paprika, coriander, fish bones, heads and trimmings and more oil if necessary, and stir together for 2 minutes. Douse with half the wine, add the tomatoes and water, thyme and the half-orange and season with salt and pepper. Cover and simmer briskly for 30 minutes until the fish has broken up and the vegetables are soft. Allow to cool. Remove the half-orange then liquidize and sieve the remainder. Reserve about 300 ml (10 fl oz) and bring the rest back to a gentle simmer.

Put the couscous in a bowl and just cover with boiling water. Allow to stand for 3-4 minutes, then fork well, adding the butter and salt and pepper. Either microwave for 2-3 minutes or heat in a covered pan, forking frequently. Cover and keep warm.

In a large pan fry the remaining vegetables and peppers until just softening. Fry the chillies then remove. Place the fish pieces on the vegetables, douse with wine and cover the pan for a few seconds. Season with salt and pepper and pour over enough of the sauce just to cover the ingredients. Heat through until just cooked, add the prawns and garnish with lots of fresh coriander.

Liquidize the chillies with reserved sauce, warm through and put in a warmed serving bowl. This will be very hot as a good contrasting flavour, but not for the fainthearted.

Serve the stew in a large warmed bowl, with the hot sauce and couscous served separately, allowing people to help themselves.

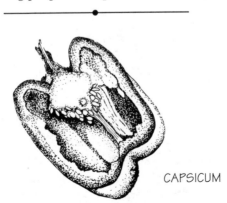

CAPSICUM

Slip Soles with Ginger and Spring Onions

The Dover sole has the most flexible, muscular body of any flat fish. It lives on rough ground, eating small shellfish, and trawlermen have to employ cunning tactics to catch the larger fish, tickling them from their habitat. Dover sole is prized for its firm, meaty flesh and exquisite texture and flavour. It is a very popular fish in restaurants, because it's easy to eat, as the very solid flesh is easy to remove from the bone.

Smaller fish, known in the trade as slips, are less expensive. In the summer and autumn they are as fat as butter, an eight ounce fish yielding a remarkable amount of flesh for its size. Two of these make an excellent meal. Cooked this way, the fish will push off the centre bone very easily and can be eaten without any fear of bones!

Serves 4 as a main course, 8 as a fish course
8 x 225 g (8 oz) slip Dover soles
1 bunch of very green spring onions
25 g (1 oz) fresh root ginger, scraped
25 g (1 oz) butter
1 tablespoon olive oil
4 tablespoons dry white wine
salt and freshly ground black pepper

Remove the skin from both sides of the sole then use kitchen scissors to 'box' the fish, removing the frill fins, cutting right back to the main frame of the fish. You can see where the bones meet by holding the fish up to the light – it is about 1 cm ($\frac{1}{2}$ in) in from the frill.

Cut the spring onions into quarters lengthways then into 5 cm (2 in) pieces. Slice the ginger into thin pieces then cut into 2.5 cm (1 in) tiny sticks. Melt half the butter with a little oil and fry the spring onions and ginger very gently for a few seconds. Add the wine and heat through.

Heat a grill tray, then brush with oil and butter. Place each fish on the tray, turning immediately to coat in hot oil. Space the fish so that they do not overlap and grill for 3-5 minutes, until the centre muscle of the fish just begins to part. Season lightly with salt and pepper, then spoon over the spring onions and ginger. Remove from the heat and allow to absorb the flavours for 1-2 minutes before transferring to a warmed serving plate with all the juices. Serve immediately.

Cuttlefish with Charred Vegetables (see page 22)

*Poached Sewin with
Sorrel Cream Sauce*
(see page 81)

*Gower Lobster with
Beurre Blanc*
(see page 74)

Pink Venison Steak Salad
(see page 147)

*Pasta with Celery and
Blue Cheese Sauce
(see page 47)*

Ragout of Lamb with Root Vegetables (see page 96) and *Couscous* (see page 130)

*Fillet of Beef with
Beetroot and Truffle*
(see page 106)

Summer Fruit Gratin
(see page 150)

Sewin (Welsh Sea Trout)

If salmon is the king of fish, sewin is the Welsh prince. It is a trout that goes to sea to feed, returning to the river to spawn. They feed more locally than salmon, and hence are more distinctive from region to region, depending on the feeding grounds. Sewin has pale, pinky flesh, with a high oil content. Fishermen say it is the most exciting fish to catch, particularly at the dead of night. Few chefs would dispute that it's one of the most palatable fish of all. The season begins around Easter and continues throughout the summer. The largest fish run earliest, but do not have the flavour of the 1-2 kg (2¼- 4½lb) fish that appear in the estuaries from May onwards. In August, small 450 g (1 lb) 'harvest' sewin can be plentiful and are delicious for a single portion.

Poached Sewin with Sorrel Cream Sauce

All village markets sell sewin when caught by netsmen or anglers. Carmarthen market is renowned for the stall of the Rees Brothers, local fishermen who regularly sell their catch. Sea trout from Scotland can be plentiful in the summer in all fishmongers, and even farmed trout make a reasonable substitute.

Serves 6
225 g (8 oz) onions, roughly chopped
100 g (4 oz) carrots, roughly chopped
1 celery stick, roughly chopped
2-3 sprigs of fresh parsley
4 bay leaves
1 sprig of fresh thyme
150 ml (5 fl oz) dry white wine or cider
2 tablespoons salt
6 black peppercorns, crushed
1.5 kg (3 lb) whole fresh sewin or a tail from a larger fish
50 g (2 oz) unsalted butter
100 g (4 oz) fresh sorrel, torn up or chopped
juice of 1 lemon
½ teaspoon cayenne
salt and freshly ground black pepper
150 ml (5 fl oz) double cream

First, make a court bouillon in a pan large enough to take fish. Place the onions, carrots and celery in the kettle with the herbs, wine or cider, salt and pepper, cover with water and simmer for 20 minutes for the flavours to develop. Add the fish, just return to a simmer, then switch off the heat and allow to stand for 20 minutes.

To make the sauce, melt the butter and fry the sorrel gently for 5-6 minutes until soft. Add the lemon juice, cayenne and a little seasoning. Add the cream and heat through, mixing well.

After 20 minutes the fish will be cooked. Remove it from the water and leave on a warmed serving plate for 5 minutes. The skin will now come off easily, but skin the top part only. Separate the fish lengthways along the lateral line, easing the pink flesh from the main backbone, and serve with sorrel sauce and new potatoes.

SALMON

Wild salmon, still frequenting many Welsh rivers, is the most romantic of fish. Hatched high in the moorlands of mid-Wales, it returns to live in the North Atlantic, where it grows at an amazing rate. By instinct, it scents its way back to its own river to spawn and continue the species. After a year at sea it will be up to 3.5 kg (8 lb) in weight, after four it could be 18 kg (40 lb). The flavour from the diet of prawns and other crustacea is sensual and exotic. It makes the centrepiece at the finest banquets, or can be filleted to make delicious individual cuts.

Farmed salmon is available from fishmongers and supermarkets throughout the year. It is probably the best value fish you can find, and some say it is indistinguishable from wild fish. But the very appearance of the 'salmo salar', the leaper, its rakish, streamlined silver body, with powerful fins and a spade of a tail to drive it up the most awesome rapids, suggests it has more muscular flesh. The texture is more solid and defined, with a paler colour than farmed, and a flavour more of wild herbs and shellfish than the more buttery farmed fish. Although in season from February to October, the main runs of fish are from June to September. However, when the fish enters the river the flesh begins to deteriorate as it converts to roe towards spawning time. A 'gravid' fish, blacker on the belly and generally thinner in shape, should be avoided, indeed should be left in the river to spawn.

PAN-FRIED WILD SALMON WITH BACON AND JUNIPER

You can poach, steam, fry, bake or grill salmon, but always take care not to overcook it, or be too aggressive, for the oil must be retained in the fish for it to remain moist. The flavour marries well with a wide range of sauces and garnishes, and this recipe works remarkably well and is very quick to make. Fillets or 'dalles' of salmon can now be bought in supermarkets or from fishmongers and have no bones at all.

Serves 4
4 x 150 g (5 oz) 'dalles' of wild salmon
2 tablespoons olive oil
50 g (2 oz) thin smoked streaky bacon, rinded and cut into 2.5 cm (1 in) pieces
50 g (2 oz) shallots, thinly sliced
12 juniper berries or green peppercorns, flattened
salt and freshly ground black pepper
150 ml (5 fl oz) very dry white wine such as Muscadet, Gros Plant or Frascati
450 g (1 lb) ripe tomatoes or 300 ml (10 fl oz) passata
2-3 sprigs of fresh basil

*T*ake the dalles from a fillet of salmon by cutting at an angle across the girth of the fish to the skin, and remove any bones with tweezers.

Heat half the oil and fry the bacon until just golden, then remove from the pan. Add the shallots and juniper berries or peppercorns and fry for 1 minute, then push them to the side of the pan. Add the salmon steaks, cooking briskly for 1 minute, then turn them over, season with salt and pepper and pile shallots and juniper on to each dalle. Top with the bacon pieces and add the wine, which will boil quickly, cover and cook on a very low heat for just a minute.

Meanwhile, liquidize the tomatoes with the basil stalks, then press through a sieve, or simply add some finely chopped basil leaves to the passata.

Using a fish slice, lift the salmon on to a warmed serving plate and keep it warm. Add the tomato and basil sauce to the pan and heat through quickly for a minute, stirring in the remaining olive oil and chopped basil leaves. Check and adjust the seasoning to taste. Serve on the side with salmon.

SALMON FISH CAKES

$\mathscr{F}$ish cakes are now so fashionable, they are the epitome of inverted snobbery and the cause for much discussion – just as other gastronauts used to debate *bouillabaisse*. Fish cakes were originally made to use up all the left-overs of fish and mashed potatoes, just as cabbage and spud made bubble and squeak. Many designer fish cakes use exotic species and shellfish. The lively textures of the fish are frequently pounded to a dead purée in a food processor and encased in a crisp flour, egg and breadcrumb shroud. Others I've tasted omit potato as being too down-market, but the flavour characters are trapped within. For a good fish cake, the mixture needs texture, even chunkiness, from the fish and potatoes, lightly flavoured with some herbs and seasoning and with a crisp outer, either from straight frying or crunchy breadcrumbs. A good home-made tartare sauce from mayonnaise and lots of chopped capers is the only accompaniment necessary; certainly not lavish shellfish sauces that turn the cakes soggy and confuse the tastes completely. The Crown Inn at Whitebrook is well placed for supplies of fresh Wye salmon, but admits without apology that it often uses farmed fish, which is frequently the best value from the fishmonger. Their fish cakes are a delicious, old-fashioned style.

Serves 4
450 g (1 lb) fresh salmon
2 leeks, finely chopped
25 g (1 oz) butter
25 g (1 oz) fresh dill, chopped
225 g (8 oz) mashed potato
salt and freshly ground black pepper
25 g (1 oz) plain flour
25 g (1 oz) fresh breadcrumbs
25 g (1 oz) maize meal
2 tablespoons seasoned flour
1 egg, beaten
olive oil

FOR THE SAUCE
2 tablespoons mayonnaise
1 tablespoon capers, roughly chopped

$\mathscr{P}$oach the salmon in water until just cooked, then drain. Fry the leeks in butter until soft. Flake the salmon and stir the flesh with the leeks and dill into the mashed potato, taking care not to break up the salmon too much. Check and adjust the seasoning to taste. Allow to cool. Shape the mixture into 8 fish cakes then chill until firm. Mix together the flour, breadcrumbs and maize meal. Dip the fish cakes in seasoned flour, then in egg, then in the crumb mixture. Heat a little oil and fry the fish cakes until golden brown on both sides and heated through. Mix together the sauce ingredients and serve with the fish cakes.

———————————•———————————

STUFFED SQUID WITH CHILLI AND INK SAUCE

Squid are remarkably plentiful in the early summer when shoals invade the coastal seas in search of prey. Other catches diminish as they flee from these predators, and hence squid become very inexpensive.
Squid have the most succulent flesh but only a very small ink sac, which dictates more delicate cookery than used for cuttlefish. They are always available frozen, often prepared, but fresh should be used whenever possible.

Serves 4
4 spring onions with lots of green
1 green pepper
4 fresh red chilli peppers
2 tablespoons extra virgin olive oil
4 garlic cloves, thinly sliced
tops of celery with lots of green, chopped
25 g (1 oz) fresh root ginger, scraped and thinly sliced
2 large sprigs of fresh parsley, chopped
salt and freshly ground black pepper
8 x 100 g (4 oz) squid, prepared, reserving the ink
200 ml (7 fl oz) dry white wine
100 g (4 oz) plum tomatoes, diced

Chop the green of the spring onions and thinly slice the remainder. Chop half the green pepper and thinly slice the remainder. Chop a little of the red chilli and thinly slice the remainder. Heat half the oil and fry the chopped spring onions, chopped pepper and chilli, half the garlic, the celery tops and a little ginger gently, until just soft, adding lots of chopped parsley and salt and pepper. Allow to cool then stuff the squid bodies with this mixture.

Heat the remaining oil and fry the remaining vegetables and chilli in the oil until softening. Cut the tentacles into 2 cm (³/₄ in) pieces, add to the pan and cook briskly for 1 minute. Douse with half the wine and boil for 1 minute, then add the tomatoes and check and adjust the seasoning. Mix the ink with the rest of the wine, stir into the sauce and simmer for 4-5 minutes.

Meanwhile, grill or grillomat the squid on both sides until they plump up and char slightly. Season and sprinkle with a little oil. Serve the tentacle and ink sauce on a plate with a pair of stuffed squid in the centre, sprinkled with the remaining parsley.

———————————————————— • ————————————————————

ROASTED WINGS OF SKATE WITH DARK VINEGAR SAUCE

Skate, or 'roker' as it's known in the trade, is landed in quantity by all larger deep-fishing trawlers. Only the wings of the fish are landed as the cartilaginous body yields little meat, except for the cheek muscles, sometimes sold as skate balls! The most plentiful is the thornback which, as its name suggests, has many ugly short spines, which are removed when it is skinned. The common ray has only a few spines, but the prized species is the blonde ray, identifiable by the total absence of thorns. The rough back skin is always removed before cooking. Skate must be eaten very fresh as it acquires a strong taste of ammonia after a few days. Tapenade, a black olive paste, is available in all good supermarkets.

Serves 4
4 x 250-300 g (9-11 oz) wings fresh skate, dark side skinned
2 tablespoons oil
100 g (4 oz) shallots, finely chopped
salt and freshly ground black pepper
4 teaspoons tapenade
2 teaspoons balsamic vinegar

Pre-heat the oven to 200ºC/400ºF/gas 6. Heat a tray in the oven for a minute, then brush the tray and fish with oil. Place the fish on the tray white skin-side down. Sprinkle the shallots over the fish and roast in the pre-heated oven for. 5-7 minutes, basting and seasoning during cooking.

Spoon off any excess juice and mix this into the tapenade with the balsamic vinegar. Pour evenly over each wing and cook for a further 2-3 minutes. Serve the fish with all the juices, mixed well.

———————————————————— • ————————————————————

SAUTÉED WHOLE PLAICE WITH CAPER MAYONNAISE

This is the most popular of flatfish, usually bought ready filleted. However, as with many fish, the flavour is very fine if cooked on the bone. Smaller plaice are too fiddly to fillet, but if totally trimmed or 'boxed' to remove all the annoying bones from the frills, the fish can be cooked and eaten with confidence. Whole plaice can be bought from fishmongers and supermarkets – look out for bargains in the autumn.

Serves 4
4 x 350 g (12 oz) fresh plaice
1 tablespoon oil
225 g (8 oz) onions, sliced
salt and freshly ground black pepper
4 teaspoons capers with their juice
2 teaspoons sun-dried tomato paste
4 tablespoons mayonnaise
1 lemon, cut into wedges

Trim the plaice by removing the head and tail with scissors. By flexing the sides of the fish you can see where the frill bones join the main frame. Cut here with scissors around the fish to 'box'. This gives thick, chunky pieces, leaving only the main backbone from which the flesh can easily be removed.

Heat the oil and fry the onions for 1 minute to colour slightly. Push to the side, add the fish to the pan dark skin side down and fry gently for 1 minute. Turn over carefully and season with salt and pepper.
Chop half the capers and mix with the onions, then cover each fish with the mixture. Cover the pan and cook for 2-3 minutes on a medium heat.

Chop the remaining capers with their juice, then mix them into the mayonnaise with the sun-dried tomato paste.

Arrange the fish and onions on a warmed serving plate and serve with the caper mayonnaise and lemon wedges.

CRAB

*W*elsh lobster fishermen catch many crabs as a by-catch or even a nuisance. But a hen crab can have the most delicately flavoured dark meat. In areas where rocks are exposed at low tide, crabs are caught under ledges and these frequently have the best, firmest meat and are very full in the shell. Hence, always select a crab that is relatively heavy for its size and has a solid, firm shell. Hen crabs have smaller claws, an arched back and a wide, egg-carrying tail that makes their appearance distinctive.

The amount of dark meat is often excessive for a straightforward crab dish, so I use it as a flavouring for fish cakes, soup, pâté and sauces. It has to be very fresh, and freezing dissipates the flavour completely.

————————————————●————————————————

*H*EN CRAB AND POLLOCK FISH CAKES WITH LEMON MAYONNAISE

*P*ollock is similar to coley, and frequently caught by anglers from boats off the coast. It has little distinction in the culinary world, but the soft flesh is fine for fish cakes. Any similar white fish – coley, whiting, codling, haddock – may be used in this recipe.

Serves 4
450 g (1 lb) hen crab, freshly boiled
900 g (2 lb) fresh pollock, gutted and de-headed
450 g (1 lb) potatoes, peeled
25 g (1 oz) butter
salt and freshly ground black pepper
2-3 large sprigs of fresh parsley, finely chopped
100 g (4 oz) fine breadcrumbs
oil for frying
150 ml (5 fl oz) mayonnaise
grated rind and juice of ½ lemon
dash of cayenne pepper

*T*o extract the best meat from the crab it must be jointed correctly. A hair grip, thin-bladed knife, or a flat-ended teaspoon handle helps scoop out the meat from the 'honeycomb' or body. A nutcracker is very useful for breaking the claws and legs. Part the back shell (carapace) from the body, removing the stomach sac from behind the jaws and the gills or sponge-like fingers, and scoop out the meat. It is best when light yellow in colour and filling the shell completely, with the new soft shell outline. Remove the legs and claws, where the base knuckle is attached to the body, to expose the honeycomb. Break each claw into its three joints. You can scoop out the meat from the bottom two parts, but the claw itself must be carefully cracked and the main sinew discarded. Break off the bottom joints of the legs, discarding the rest. Crack the leg joint with a nutcracker to expose the meat. Reserve the white meat in large flakes and slice the brown meat to 5 mm ($1/_4$ in) pieces.

Bake, grill, or poach the pollock very lightly then allow to cool, remove the skin and bones and lightly flake the flesh.

Meanwhile, cut the potatoes into about 2.5 cm (1 in) even pieces, cover with water and simmer until just soft. Drain and mash, adding butter and salt and pepper. Fold in the pollock and crab with the parsley and seasoning, mixing carefully so as not to break up flakes too much. Leave for 30 minutes. Shape the mixture into 6 x 2 cm ($2^1/_2$ x $^3/_4$ in) round cakes then coat with breadcrumbs, pressing in well. Heat the frying oil and shallow fry the fish cakes for 2 minutes on either side until golden.

Mix the mayonnaise with the lemon zest and juice and cayenne. Serve on the side with the fish cakes.

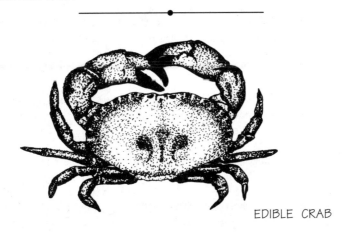

EDIBLE CRAB

CRAB STEW WITH HERBS, CIDER AND PASTA

*T*his dish may be a little messy to eat, like devouring the juicy crab in ginger at a Chinese restaurant, but the flavour makes it worthwhile. If you can't buy live crabs, use freshly boiled ones and decrease the cooking time by half.

Serves 4
4 tablespoons oil
225 g (8 oz) onions, sliced
4 garlic cloves, lightly crushed
1 red pepper, thickly sliced
2 celery sticks, thickly sliced
4 x 450 g (1 lb) live hen crabs
1 large bunch of fresh herbs such as fennel, rosemary, thyme and bay
1.2 litres (2 pints) very dry cider
450 g (1 lb) tin tomatoes or fresh tomatoes
rind of ½ orange
salt and freshly ground black pepper
225 g (8 oz) fresh pasta such as linguine or tagliatelle

*H*eat the oil in a large pan and fry the onions, garlic, pepper and celery over a brisk heat until just colouring on the edges.

Using a very heavy knife, chop the crabs in half by turning them on their backs and cutting through the tail. Crack the claws, retaining all the juices. Remove the stomach sac and pull the body shell away to reveal the 'fingers' or gills which can easily be removed. They are not poisonous but are unpalatable.

Add the crabs to the pan and mix well with the vegetables. Add the herbs in large sprigs. Cover the pan and cook together for 2-3 minutes, shaking the pan frequently. Add cider and continue cooking for 5 minutes, by which time all the crab shells should have turned bright in colour. Add the tomatoes, orange peel, all the juices and seasoning, cover and simmer gently for 15-20 minutes.

Using a slotted spoon, transfer all the crab pieces to a warmed serving platter and keep them warm. Discard the herbs and orange peel then add the pasta to the liquid. Check the seasoning, adding a little more cider if necessary. Simmer for 5 minutes until the pasta is almost cooked.

Serve the pasta and liquid in bowls, and give the guests nutcrackers and picks to extract the meat from the crabs.

*F*ILLET OF GREY MULLET WITH FENNEL AND TOMATO

*T*his beautiful, silvery-grey fish is very plentiful in all estuaries, but very elusive to fishermen. However, many are caught in salmon nets and the seine nets that now entangle the coast. Its quality was exposed by the ethnic community who often use it as an alternative to the expensive sea bass. At a fraction of the price, it has beautiful, firm, white meat. But it must be cleaned when very fresh, as its grubbing feeding fashion turns the innards very quickly. Mullet can be baked whole, just as the traditional local recipes for bass, but the fillets, totally boned, are particularly fine. You can ask your fishmonger to fillet the fish for you once you have selected very fresh ones!

Serves 4
1.5-1.75 kg (34 lb) fresh grey mullet
2 tablespoons oil
salt and freshly ground black pepper
1 small bunch of fresh fennel, finely chopped
225 g (8 oz) fresh tomatoes
50 g (2 oz) shallots, finely chopped
2 tablespoons extra virgin olive oil
1 teaspoon balsamic vinegar

*S*cale, gut and quickly wash the grey mullet. To remove the fillets, place the fish flat on a board and, using a sturdy, sharp knife, cut horizontally from the dorsal fin along the backbone to the tail. Cut back to the head, removing the meat carefully from the cavity bones, but do not bother with the flank or belly meat. Repeat for the other side to give two long fillets. Cut each fillet in half to give four equal portions

Heat a tray under the grill, then lightly oil and place the fish skin-side down, basting the top with hot oil. Grill for 2-3 minutes, basting a few times and seasoning lightly with salt and pepper. When the fish is just cooked, test for firmness by pressing with the flat of a knife. Sprinkle with half the fennel and keep it warm.

Make the sauce by liquidizing then sieving the tomatoes. Add the shallots and remaining fennel, olive oil, balsamic vinegar and salt and pepper. Mix well and just warm through.

Serve the fish on warmed plates surrounded by the sauce.

———————————●———————————

ROAST MONKFISH IN SMOKED BACON
WITH RED WINE AND THYME SAUCE

Monkfish, lotte and rape are all familiar European names for the angler fish. This is a very ugly, bottom-living brute that catches other fish by waving a spiny fin on the end of its nose to entice them near its enormous mouth. Although it sounds more like a modern horror movie, this top of the tree, cartilaginous carnivore has the most wonderful tail flesh with no spindly bones at all. The texture is solid without grain or flakiness, making it perfect for kebabs. The French call it *gigot de mer,* as a large tail can be roasted just like a leg of lamb!

The true monkfish, known to fishermen as fiddlefish, is a relative of the shark, sandpaper-skinned with a flattened head and skate-like front fins. The flesh is also very good and inexpensive, as the preparation is more tedious, but nevertheless worthwhile if a trawlerman offers you a fiddle for nothing. Monkfish is now seen in every fish shop and supermarket. This dish from Dolmelynllyn Hall overlooking Cardigan Bay cooks it French-style, with an unusual red wine sauce that marries well with the solid texture of the fish. Instead of the thyme garnish, you might like to try toasted walnut halves and baby onions that have been cooked in a light stock then caramelized in butter and brown sugar.

Serves 2
2 x 175 g (6 oz) monkfish fillets, skinned
1 garlic clove, crushed
300 ml (10 fl oz) red wine
3 large sprigs of fresh thyme
2 tablespoons walnut oil
4 rashers smoked bacon, rinded
50 g (2 oz) butter
150 ml (5 fl oz) water
25 g (1 oz) plain flour

Pre-heat the oven to 180ºC/350ºF/gas 4. Marinate the monkfish in the garlic, half the wine, two of the sprigs of thyme and the walnut oil for 2 hours. Remove from the marinade. Put the bacon between two pieces of cling film and bat until thin, then roll around the marinated fish.

Melt half the butter in a small roasting tray until sizzling. Add the fish, turning to coat in the butter, then put into the pre-heated oven for 10 minutes. Remove and keep warm.

Meanwhile, put the marinade into a pan with the remaining wine and the water and boil until reduced by half. Cream the remaining butter with the flour and gradually whisk into the sauce until thick. Reserve the tops of the thyme for garnish, strip the rest and add it to the sauce. Add a little more water if the consistency is too thick.

Slice the fish into four or five pieces. Spoon some of the sauce on to warmed plates and arrange the fish on top. Garnish with the reserved thyme.

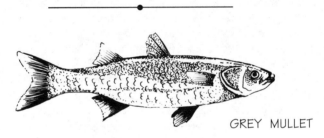

GREY MULLET

Main Courses - Meat

Welsh Lamb

The banner on Welsh lamb enjoys international recognition. Few gourmets would dispute the quality of the new spring lamb in the markets from May each year. Similarly the autumn lamb, which acquires a stronger gamey flavour, is rich and delicious.

But the terrain where lambs are reared varies greatly. In west Wales the sea spray flavours the goose grass of cliffs where sheep graze. The brackish, muddy estuaries sprout samphire and seabeet on the salt marshes, which are always speckled white with lambs. These areas produce very different meat from the windswept heathlands, mauve with summer heathers at two thousand feet higher in Snowdonia. Mountain lamb will taste more aromatic, whereas marsh lamb is very rich from the salty vegetation.

In Normandy, salt marsh lamb, known as *pré-salé* lamb is a great speciality, particularly around the famous abbey of Mont St Michel. It is not sold with the same distinction in Wales. But local butchers will be able to advise you on the origin of the lamb, whether mountain, farm or salt marsh. In a supermarket you can distinguish the degree of maturity by the lightness of the lean and the covering of fat. As the lamb grows, the meat darkens as the animal puts on more fat, hence it has the stronger flavour.

In Wales, the cooks are presented with very individual flavours in every region, which also vary as the seasons progress. Young lamb has sweet and mild-flavoured offal that is ideal for a light spring casserole, particularly if warmth of flavour is still required in a meal for a cold April day.

Minted Leg of Lamb with Sea Salt Crust

Wild mint grows all around the coast of Wales and is found in abundance on the edge of salt marshes. The Mawddach and Dovey estuaries have large *pré-salé* areas where sheep are grazed, acquiring the rich saline nuances in the flesh. Dolmelynllyn Hall is a beautiful old stone manor in Cader Idris in the heart of the hill lamb country. Their roasted leg in a salt crust brings some of the sea air flavour to the herbiness of the hillside grazings.

Serves 8-10
2.5-2.75 kg (5-6 lb) leg of Welsh lamb, boned and rolled
2 garlic cloves, sliced
1 bunch of fresh mint
salt and freshly ground black pepper
750 g (1½ lb) plain flour
50 g (2 oz) sea salt
50 g (2 oz) butter, softened
4 teaspoons concentrated mint sauce
600 ml (1 pint) lamb stock
50 ml (2 fl oz) dry sherry
1 teaspoon cornflour (optional)

Pre-heat the oven to 220ºC / 425ºF / gas 7. Make 12 cuts in the lamb, put a slice of garlic and a mint leaf into each cut and season with salt and pepper. Roast in the pre-heated oven for 40 minutes, then remove and allow to cool.

Sift the flour into a large bowl, add the sea salt and gradually add enough cold water to mix to a fairly stiff dough. Chill for 30 minutes. Roll out the dough until it is big enough to fit the lamb and overlap. Mix the butter with the mint sauce, spread over the top of the lamb, leaving any remaining juices in the dish. Place the lamb upside down on the pastry, folding the sides of the dough over and making sure there are no holes. Place the lamb back in the roasting tin and roast in the oven for 40 minutes for pink or up to 1½ hours for well done.

Put the stock in a pan and add the juice left from the mint paste. Add the sherry, bring to the boil and boil until reduced by half. Reserve a few top sprigs of mint for garnish, strip the rest, finely chop the leaves and add to the gravy. If the gravy is too thin, thicken with a little cornflour mixed with water. Check and adjust the seasoning if necessary.

When the lamb is cooked, remove it from the oven, cut all around the pastry, remove the top and discard it. Scrape the mint residue from the top and add it to the gravy. Remove the lamb from the rest of the pastry, place on a carving board and cut into thick slices. Pour some of the gravy on to warmed plates, arrange the lamb on top and garnish with the mint sprigs.

————————————— • —————————————

RAGOUT OF LAMB WITH ROOT VEGETABLES

*T*his recipe uses the liver, kidneys, sweetbreads and heart, but you can omit these and use an extra 350 g (12 oz) of lean lamb if you prefer to use just lean meat. You could serve this with the couscous from the *Vegetable and Tomato Casserole with Couscous* (see page 130).

Serves 4-6
350 g (12 oz) diced lean lamb
175 g (6 oz) liver, cut into small, thin slices
100 g (4 oz) kidneys, trimmed and quartered
100 g (4 oz) neck sweetbreads, diced
1 heart, trimmed and sliced
2 tablespoons oil
salt and freshly ground black pepper
200 g (8 oz) shallots
100 g (4 oz) small turnips
100 g (4 oz) small carrots
1 small celery heart
1 teaspoon fresh thyme leaves
300 ml (10 fl oz) dry country cider
300 ml (10 fl oz) tomato juice
1 teaspoon mustard
2 tablespoons chopped fresh parsley

*V*ery quickly fry the meats individually in a little oil in a very hot pan until lightly browned, then reserve them together, seasoning well with salt and pepper.

Cut vegetables into 2.5 cm (1 in) sticks and thin slices in varying shapes for interesting presentation. Cook them quickly in a little oil to soften, then add the meats to the pan with the fresh thyme and heat through. Douse with cider and boil over a high heat to evaporate the cider very quickly. Mix together the tomato juice and mustard, add to the pan and heat through for 2-3 minutes to form a rich sauce with the lightly cooked meats. Sprinkle generously with parsley and serve.

ℒAMB HOTPOT WITH TOMATOES AND FLAGEOLETS

𝒯his quick lamb casserole has a fresh flavour as the acidity of the tomatoes counteracts the slight fattiness of the lamb. It is a complete dish as the creamy, waxy texture of the beans contrasts with the juicy chunks of lamb in the rich sauce.

Serves 4
1 tablespoon olive oil
6 plump shallots, halved
4 garlic cloves, crushed
450 g (1 lb) lean lamb, cut into 3 cm (1 in) dice
salt and freshly ground black pepper
250 ml (8 fl oz) fruity red wine, Beaujolais or similar
3 sprigs of fresh rosemary
450 g (1 lb) tin chopped tomatoes
450 g (1 lb) tin flageolet beans
2 large sprigs of fresh parsley, chopped

𝒫re-heat the oven to 180ºC/350ºF/gas 4. Heat the oil in a flameproof casserole and fry the shallots quickly until coloured on the edges. Add the garlic and meat, cooking rapidly and stirring continuously, so that it colours quickly. Season generously with salt and pepper, then add the red wine and boil rapidly. Add the rosemary sprigs, tomatoes and beans. Cover and cook in the pre-heated oven for about 45 minutes until the meat is tender. Top with freshly chopped parsley and serve.

———————————●———————————

GARLIC

STUFFED SHOULDER OF AUTUMN LAMB
WITH WILD MUSHROOMS

The shoulder of lamb is very succulent as it has a higher fat content than the leg. However, it is difficult to carve, so shops often sell it already boned and rolled. This recipe cooks the meat without any confining string, so the muscles form to their natural shape, using a stuffing made from the trimmings to replace the bones in the centre of the meat. It carves into neat slices which present very well on the plate.

If you have a local butcher he will 'barrel bone' this joint for you, keeping the cavity for the stuffing, and chop the bones. A supermarket boned and rolled shoulder can be untied and reshaped. You may need to skewer it to hold in the stuffing.

Lamb in the autumn has a stronger flavour and is greatly enhanced by fresh, wild mushrooms that grow in a moist, warm atmosphere. The mellow fruity flavour of wild ceps, chanterelles or field mushrooms is particularly distinctive.

Serves 6-8
2.25-2.75 kg (56 lb) shoulder of lamb, boned
1 tablespoon oil
225 g (8 oz) shallots, chopped
2 celery sticks, chopped
225 g (8 oz) carrots, chopped
225 g (8 oz) small swede, chopped
225 g (8 oz) field mushrooms or chanterelles or ceps, if possible, sliced
salt and freshly ground black pepper
8 garlic cloves, unpeeled
1 large sprig of fresh rosemary
600 ml (1 pint) dark beer
300 ml (10 fl oz) stock
25 ml (1 fl oz) dry Madeira or sherry

Pre-heat the oven to 230ºC/450ºF/gas 8. Trim the neck and foreleg parts of the joint and reserve all the trimmings to make up about 200 g (7 oz) in weight. Heat the oil and fry about 225 g (8 oz) of the chopped vegetables - shallots, celery, carrots and swede - until soft. Add about half the mushrooms and heat through, then leave to cool.

Chop the meat trimmings in a food processor for a few seconds then remove. Finely chop the cooked vegetables in the processor. Add half the meat trimmings in small quantities and grind finely. Add the rest of the meat trimmings and mix for just a few seconds to retain a chunkier texture. Season well with salt and pepper.

Press this stuffing into the cavity of the joint so it spreads throughout the entire part where the bones were removed. Slightly flatten with your hand to form it to an even thickness. Leave in a cool place for at least 1 hour, or chill until ready to roast. Note the joint is not tied at all, but may be skewered at the edges if necessary to keep the stuffing in place.

If available, put the chopped bones with remaining vegetables in a roasting tray. Add the unpeeled garlic and rosemary and place meat on top, skin uppermost. With a sharp knife or Stanley knife, lightly score the fat in a 1 cm ($^1/_2$ in) criss-cross pattern. Lightly oil. Place in the pre-heated oven for 30 minutes. The meat will plump up as it takes its natural shape. Spoon the pan juices over the meat and season generously, then continue to cook for a further 30-50 minutes. Ensure the fat doesn't burn, and baste several times as the flavours from the vegetables mingle with the meat and juices. Increase the cooking time if you prefer lamb well done. Transfer the meat to a tray and keep warm for at least 30 minutes before carving. During this time the cooking subsides and the juices 'set' in the meat, keeping it moist.

Make the gravy by pouring off the fat from the roasting tray. Add the beer and boil for 5 minutes to mix the flavours. Add the stock and simmer for 15 minutes, squeezing the juices from all the vegetables. If you like a thick gravy, liquidize some of the vegetables with the stock, particularly the garlic and shallots, for after the time spent cooking, the sharp, strong flavours will have become sweet and creamy.

Thinly slice the remaining mushrooms and gently fry in a little oil until soft. Add the Madeira or sherry and simmer for 2-3 minutes. Sieve the gravy into the pan with the mushrooms, check and adjust the seasoning and keep hot.

Carve the meat in vertical slices from the open end where the stuffing will be bulging out. Each slice should show the lean meat on the outside with the stuffing in the centre. Serve two slices per person with gravy on the side.

———————●———————

Welsh Beef

Traditional Welsh black beef cattle, like the natives, were small dark animals, but with exceptional strength. They foraged for a wide variety of foods and hence developed very flavoursome meat. Although much of lowland Wales is best known for dairy cattle, the vales of Glamorgan, Carmarthen, Pembroke and Anglesey, with their fine pastures, produce exceptional quality beef. Smithfield Show champions have been reared in Anglesey.
Welsh black beef, because it has a good mature flavour, is once again being reared around Wales, particularly in Pembrokeshire and Anglesey. Recently a Welsh Black Beef Society and Welsh Beef Promotions have been formed to promote fine beef from the principality.

•

Rare Roast Beef Hare and Hounds

When purchasing beef, look for flesh that is darker with speckles of fat in the lean. This is called 'marbling' and keeps the meat naturally moist and juicy during cooking. A roast rib of beef, almost black on the outside and red, juicy and succulent inside, is a meal hard to better. However, only a large joint produces this exceptional succulence, for smaller pieces become overcooked by the time the outside is well browned, and it is best to plan a great occasion around a hearty chunk of beef.

Serves a party of 10 or more
4 kg (9 lb) joint of sirloin with rib bones
2 tablespoons hot Dijon or English mustard
2 tablespoons soft unrefined demerara sugar
550 g (1¼ lb) small onions
200 g (8 oz) carrots, roughly chopped
3 celery sticks, roughly chopped
200 g (8 oz) onions, roughly chopped
2 tablespoons oil
sea salt and freshly ground black pepper
300 ml (10 fl oz) red wine
300 ml (10 fl oz) stock

Pre-heat the oven to 240°C/475°F/gas 9. Prepare the beef by allowing it to stand at room temperature for 1-2 hours. With a sharp knife or Stanley knife, cut a 2.5 cm (1 in) deep incision the length of the loin where the end bone and fat join. Cut a diagonal 1 cm ($^1/_2$ in) wide criss-cross pattern half way through the outer fat. Spread mustard all over the fat then sprinkle with sugar to stick to the mustard.

Reserve the small onions unpeeled. Place the carrots, celery and chopped onions in a large roasting tray. Drizzle with a little oil and place the joint, fat uppermost, on top. Roast in the very hot oven for 30 minutes, ensuring the sugar doesn't brown.

Add the small onions in their husks to the tray and baste the meat well, seasoning with salt and pepper. Cook for a further 30 minutes, removing the small, whole onions when they are soft and beginning to collapse. Continue cooking the meat for a further 30 minutes. If you like meat less rare, lower the oven temperature to 190ºC/375ºF/gas 5 and continue cooking for a further 30 minutes for medium, or 1 hour for medium to well done. When cooked as desired, remove the meat and allow it to set in a warm place for at least 30 minutes.

Pour off the fat from the vegetables, add the red wine and boil until reduced by half. Add the stock and simmer for 20 minutes, ensuring all the burnt brown pieces are mixed well into the gravy. If you like a thick gravy, liquidize the vegetables then rub them through a sieve, otherwise strain the juices and serve as a thinner gravy.

Carve the meat by first cutting through a long incision down to the bones to loosen the meat, then slice the meat across the grain at 90 degrees through the crisp fat to the pink juicy centre of the eye. Serve with the roasted onions cut in half and the gravy, with fresh vegetables and potatoes.

————————————•————————————

STEAK WITH OYSTER SAUCE

This classic Victorian dish was probably heavy on oysters and light on beef, as oysters were so cheap. Indeed, about 70 oyster smacks fished from Mumbles in the late nineteenth century, annually landing in excess of fifty million oysters, making the village one of the biggest oyster fisheries in Europe. Many of these were sent to the cities of the Midlands and to London, and the oyster 'hoisters' used to cry, 'Oysters, oysters, a penny the lot!' They certainly were the food of the poor, but provided generous doses of protein and minerals to the diet. William Ewart Gladstone, the Victorian prime minister, visited Mumbles on many occasions and always partook of a feast of oysters. The Old Gladstone Restaurant remained until a few decades ago and was renowned for its 'carpetbag steaks' which combined steak with oysters. This delivers a double punch with a rich oyster sauce as an accompaniment. You can use more oysters for the sauce if your guests are fans of these molluscs. A similar dish can be made using mussels, prawns or king prawns, or even white crabmeat. All are variations on the 'surf and turf' theme.

For those who prefer the light meats, use chicken breast instead of steak. The combination with crab or mussels is particularly successful. Be sure to cook the chicken for longer until it is firm and cooked through.

Serves 4
4 x 175 g (6 oz) fillet or rump steak about 2.5 cm (1 in) thick
8 oysters, shelled and juice reserved
salt and freshly ground black pepper

FOR THE SAUCE
25 g (1 oz) butter
juice of ½ lemon
2 egg yolks
150 ml (5 fl oz) single cream
dash of Worcestershire sauce
pinch of cayenne pepper

Prepare the steaks by making an incision into the side of each steak and filling with an oyster. Cook on a grillomat or in a heavy-based pan or under a grill for 2-3 minutes on either side, seasoning with salt and generously with freshly ground black pepper. Once the steaks are just coloured brown but still rare they are perfect, as overcooking dries the meat.

Meanwhile, make the sauce by melting the butter in a small pan with the oyster and lemon juice. Add the remaining oysters for a few seconds just to heat through and firm slightly. Whisk together the egg yolks and cream and swirl in, cooking for a few seconds to thicken slightly without allowing the mixture to boil. Add the Worcestershire sauce and cayenne and spoon the sauce on to warmed plates. Put each steak into the centre, top with an oyster and a little sauce and cayenne and serve.

NATIVE OYSTERS

WELSH BLACK STEAK WITH TWO MUSTARD SAUCES

Good Welsh black beef steak has been well hung as part of the agreed *modus operandi* among the Welsh Black Beef Society, who pride themselves on their highest quality beef products. The steak has such a good flavour that it is criminal to marinate or drench it with garlic and other aromats, but a mild mustardy sauce that does not overpower is most acceptable. You can serve the steak with either or both the sauces below, but serve them on the side not over the meat.

Depending on the thickness of the meat it will gradually firm during cooking. Rare steaks should be just firm on the outside but with plenty of give when pressed gently. When a few beads of pinky juices appear on the meat, the heat is driving the juice right through the steak and it is becoming medium cooked. As more juice appears, so the meat will become well cooked. The best flavour is obviously when all juice is retained within the meat and hence the steak is on the rare side. If you are a well-done steak person, try taking it a little less cooked with less juice appearing on the top and, gradually, I'm sure you'll come to appreciate the flavour that should be retained in the meat.

It is also important to rest the steak for a short while before eating, so the temperature drops and no steam billows out when the meat is cut. This steam is juice which should be kept in for the best taste.

Serves 4
4 x 225 g (8 oz) sirloin, rump or fillet steaks
salt and freshly ground black pepper
2 teaspoons oil

FOR SAUCE 1
1 tablespoon made English mustard
1 tablespoon dry sherry
3 tablespoons stock
3 tablespoons fresh tomato juice

FOR SAUCE 2
1 tablespoon Meaux grain mustard
1 tablespoon tarragon vinegar
50 g (2 oz) butter
3 tablespoons fresh tomato juice

*L*ightly oil a grillomat or heavy-based pan over a low heat, gradually increasing the heat until the smoke begins to burn off. Very lightly oil the meat and place on the pan, but do not squash it during cooking as you will squeeze out the juices you need to retain within the meat. Season with salt and pepper. Cook for about 2 minutes until well browned then turn the meat using a fish slice and brown the other side, cooking until the steak is done to your liking.

Mix together the mustard sauce ingredients in separate pans, stirring so that the mustard is diluted and will freely emulsify with the other ingredients when heated through.

HERBS

$\mathscr{F}$ILLET OF BEEF WITH BEETROOT AND TRUFFLE

$\mathscr{P}$ortmeirion Hotel is flamboyant in decor and atmosphere. The new young chef, Craig Hindley, puts a similar feel into his cooking, using local ingredients dressed up with the finest relishes and garnishes, most suitable for special occasions. Most of the preparation can be done well in advance, so only the final cooking of the steak is necessary. The beetroot, a root vegetable that extracts the minerals from the soil to produce the dark crimson red flesh and rich flavours, combines well with dark meats and game. This dish is delicious served with the *Shallots Glazed in Red Wine* (see page 138).

Serves 6
675 g (1½ lb) beef fillet, trimmed of fat and sinew
salt and freshly ground black pepper

FOR THE SAUCE
25 g (1 oz) unsalted butter
8 shallots, chopped
2 garlic cloves, chopped
1 sprig of fresh thyme
1 tablespoon balsamic vinegar
200 ml (7 fl oz) port
100 ml (3½ fl oz) red wine
250 ml (8 fl oz) chicken stock
250 ml (8 fl oz) veal stock
chopped truffle (optional)
salt and freshly ground black pepper
100 g (4 oz) cooked beetroot, diced
1 teaspoon chopped fresh parsley

FOR THE GARNISH
12 shallots
1 tablespoon oil
200 ml (7 fl oz) red wine
25 g (1 oz) butter
25 g (1 oz) sugar
350 g (12 oz) puy lentils, cooked

$\mathscr{T}$o make the sauce, melt a little of the butter in a heavy-based pan and fry the shallots until beginning to soften. Add the garlic and thyme but do not allow them to colour. Add the balsamic vinegar and cook until dry. Add the port and wine and boil until reduced to one-third of the original quantity. Add the stocks and boil until reduced to half the quantity. Add the truffle, if using, whisk in the remaining butter and season with salt and pepper.

Either pre-heat the oven to 230°C/450°F/gas 8 and season and roast the beef for 15-20 minutes. Keep warm and slice into eight equal pieces just before serving. Or, cut the beef fillet into four equal pieces and season with salt and pepper. Fry quickly on both sides until lightly browned and cooked as required. Keep warm.

Meanwhile, for the garnish, fry the whole shallots in a little oil until lightly browned. Add the red wine, butter and sugar, cover and cook for 10 minutes until soft. Add the lentils and heat through, stirring. Spoon some of the lentils into the centre of four warmed plates and top each with some slices of beef and three shallots. Keep warm.

Before serving, add the beetroot and parsley to the sauce and warm through. Check and adjust the seasoning if necessary. Spoon around the beef and serve.

CRISPY BELLY PORK WITH HERBS AND GARLIC

*T*he farmyard pig has been traditional in Wales for centuries. Pork is very good value and widely available. The least expensive part of pork 'cig moch' is the belly, which traditionally was cured for bacon by all farmhouses in Wales. The crackling from this cut, if cooked to an ultimate crispiness, makes it the most succulent part of pork, rejoicing when riotous herby flavours combine with the sweet meat.

Serves 6
225 g (8 oz) carrots
450 g (1 lb) onions
1 large red pepper
12 garlic cloves
1 tablespoon oil
1 generous bunch of fresh thyme
1 generous bunch of fresh fennel
1 generous bunch of fresh rosemary
1 generous bunch of fresh sage
1.5 kg (3 lb) belly pork in one piece, skin on and bones removed
salt and freshly ground black pepper
300 ml (10 fl oz) dry farmhouse cider
150 ml (5 fl oz) pineapple juice
300 ml (10 fl oz) stock or water

*P*re-heat the oven to 230ºC/450ºF/gas 8. Roughly chop the onions, carrots and pepper into about 2.5 cm (1 in) chunks and place in a roasting tray with the garlic cloves and a little oil. Place in the pre-heated oven for 10 minutes until lightly browned.

Roughly chop herbs and sprinkle over the vegetables, then lay the belly pork on top with the skin uppermost. Lightly oil the meat then cook in the pre-heated oven for 20-30 minutes for the skin to crackle. Baste well with the juices, then season generously with salt and pepper. Continue cooking for a further 30 minutes, ensuring the skin does not burn. Cover it lightly with foil once it is very crackly.

Remove the meat from the pan and keep it warm, allowing it to set. Pour off the fatty oil from the pan and douse the vegetables with cider, then add pineapple juice and enough stock or water to just cover the vegetables. Simmer for 10-20 minutes until the vegetables are soft, then leave to cool. Remove the woody parts of the herbs then liquidize everything, pressing it through a sieve to form a highly flavoured sauce. Check and adjust the seasoning to taste.

Carve the pork by placing it on a board, crackling side down, and with a heavy knife cut vertically through meat and crackling into 1 cm ($\frac{1}{2}$ in) slices. Serve a few slices to each person with sauce on the side.

———————————•———————————

$\mathscr{F}$ILLET OF PORK WITH SPICED TURNIPS AND APPLE

$\mathcal{T}$enderloin of pork is like a pale, mini-fillet of beef. It's the bi-product of the bacon industry and hence quite reasonably priced with little waste. It is most tender and cooks very quickly. Apple sauce is very conventional with roast pork. The spiced turnips make a great foil for the blander taste of this lighter meat. Make up the spice mixture and use a quantity to suit your taste.

Serves 4
FOR THE SPICE MIXTURE
1 teaspoon allspice
1 teaspoon ground ginger
1 teaspoon ground clove
1 teaspoon ground coriander

4 x 250 g (9 oz) pork fillets
salt and freshly ground black pepper
1 tablespoon chopped fresh parsley
2 tablespoons duck fat
75 ml (3 fl oz) dry white wine
150 ml (5 fl oz) chicken stock
150 ml (5 fl oz) double cream
1 teaspoon chopped fresh tarragon

FOR THE GARNISH
20 baby turnips
2 teaspoons sugar
100 g (4 oz) butter
2 apples, skinned and cut into 20 wedges

Pre-heat the oven to 230°C/450°F/gas 8. Mix together the spice mixture ingredients.

Season the pork with salt and pepper and roll in chopped parsley. Heat the fat in a flameproof casserole and fry the pork briskly until sealed on both sides, then place in the pre-heated oven for 8-10 minutes until cooked.

Meanwhile, trim the turnips, place in a pan, barely cover with water, add a little salt, the sugar and half the butter, bring to the boil and simmer gently until just tender. Drain and keep warm.

Remove the pork from the casserole and keep it warm. Add the wine and cook over a high heat until syrupy. Add the chicken stock and boil until reduced by half. Add the cream and simmer for 1 minute until thick. Add the tarragon and check and adjust the seasoning if necessary.

Heat the remaining butter until it starts to foam. Add the apples and cook for 30 seconds. Add the turnips, season with spice mixture to taste and heat through.

Slice the pork and arrange in the centre of warmed plates. Spoon over the sauce and surround with turnips and apple.

––––––––––●––––––––––

Main Courses - Poultry and Game

Chicken with Riesling and Rosemary

*T*his is adapted from Ann Owston's rabbit recipe as served in Jemima's in west Wales. The clean flavour of Riesling makes a light yet well balanced sauce to complement the delicate flavour of chicken or rabbit. Either can be used, particularly legs of chicken and the fores of rabbit, or a combination of both.

Serves 4
4 chicken legs, skinned
salt and freshly ground white pepper
25 g (1 oz) butter
2 teaspoons oil
225 g (8 oz) onions, finely chopped
1 celery stick, sliced
2 teaspoons plain flour
450 ml (15 fl oz) Riesling wine
150 ml (5 fl oz) chicken stock
3 large sprigs of fresh rosemary
120 ml (4 fl oz) cream
2 teaspoons mustard blended with a little wine
2 teaspoons chopped fresh parsley

*S*eason the chicken legs. Heat the butter with a dash of oil and fry the chicken until golden. Remove from the pan. Add the onions and celery, sprinkle with a little flour to absorb the fat then add the wine, stirring. Bring to the boil, stirring, then return the chicken legs to the pan and add just enough stock to cover. Add two sprigs of rosemary and simmer gently for about 30 minutes until tender. Discard the rosemary. Check and adjust the seasoning to taste. Stir in the cream and mustard to thicken the sauce. Transfer to a warmed serving dish and garnish with fresh rosemary and parsley.

BAKED CHICKEN WITH GARLIC AND VEGETABLES

This is a simple but delicious recipe that you can make using a whole chicken or chicken pieces.

Serves 4
2 kg (4½ lb) chicken or chicken pieces
225 g (8 oz) onions or shallots, roughly chopped
3 tablespoons olive oil
8 garlic cloves, unpeeled
1 red pepper, seeded and cut into 8
1 green pepper, seeded and cut into 8
350 g (12 oz) aubergine, cut into 2 cm (¾ in) rings
3 large sprigs of fresh thyme or ½ teaspoon dried thyme
3 large sprigs of fresh marjoram or ½ teaspoon dried marjoram
salt and freshly ground black pepper
200 ml (7 fl oz) dry white wine
1 ciabatta loaf or French stick

Pre-heat the oven to 230ºC/450ºF/gas 8. Cut the chicken into eight pieces by cutting it in half from the neck to the parson's nose, right through the bones. Separate the leg joints and cut each leg in half through the joint. Cut the breasts into two from the wing bone to the thin end of the meat. Discard any excess fat.

Spread the onions or shallots over the bottom of a large roasting tray and pour over just enough olive oil to coat them. Put into the pre-heated oven for 5 minutes while you prepare the other vegetables.

Put the whole garlic into the tray and arrange the chicken pieces, skin-side up, in the tray. Surround with peppers and herbs, putting the aubergine around the edge of the tray. Drizzle all over with olive oil. Cook in the oven for 20 minutes. Baste well and season with salt and pepper. Cook for a further 20 minutes until the chicken is cooked through and golden and the vegetables are well browned on the edges.

Arrange the chicken, vegetables and herbs on a warmed serving platter and pour off the excess fat (retaining this to use in a risotto or with other vegetables). Pour in the wine and heat through for a few minutes, scraping off any caramelized pieces to enrich the sauce. Whisk in the remaining olive oil and pour over the chicken. Heat the bread for a minute in the oven and eat the garlic cloves pressed into slices or chunks of bread.

SUPREME OF CHICKEN WITH BEETROOT

*T*he Café Niçoise restaurant in Colwyn Bay gives a French feel to foods from north Wales as typified in this, one of their original recipes.

Serves 4
4 x 175 g (6 oz) chicken breasts, skinned
salt and freshly ground black pepper
1 tablespoon olive oil
2 shallots, finely chopped
150 ml (5 fl oz) white wine
450 ml (15 fl oz) chicken or vegetable stock
175 g (6 oz) butter
100 g (4 oz) cooked beetroot, cut into 1 cm (½ in) strips
4 fresh basil leaves, finely chopped

*P*re-heat the oven to 200ºC/400ºF/gas 6. Season the chicken breasts with salt and pepper. Heat a little oil in a flameproof casserole and fry the chicken until lightly browned. Transfer to the pre-heated oven and roast for 10-15 minutes until just firm. Remove from the casserole and keep warm. Add the shallots and wine to the casserole and simmer for 2 minutes until syrupy. Add the stock and boil until reduced by half.

Melt a little butter and fry the beetroot for a few minutes. Pour over the chicken breasts. Finish the sauce by adding the remaining butter and the basil. Spoon the sauce around the chicken and serve.

ROAST TURKEY WITH CHIPOLATAS AND CHESTNUT STUFFING

This is a real festive dish for a family party, but you can make a smaller version with chicken for a delicious dinner. Free-range birds give by far the best flavour. It is best if you can make the stuffing in advance. Serve the turkey with roast potatoes, fresh vegetables such as sprouts, carrots, parsnip and swede, bread sauce and cranberry jelly.

Serves 10
225 g (8 oz) onions, roughly chopped
225 g (8 oz) carrots, sliced lengthways
100 g (4 oz) celery, thinly sliced
1 teaspoon dried mixed Italian herbs
1 tablespoon oil
salt and freshly ground black pepper
7-7½ kg (15-17 lb) turkey
1 kg (2¼ lb) chipolata sausages
225 g (8 oz) bacon rashers, rinded
1 kg (2¼ lb) par-boiled potatoes, cut into 5 cm (2 in) pieces
300 ml (10 fl oz) dry cider
450 ml (1 pint) stock made from the turkey giblets
1 tablespoon gravy granules

FOR THE STUFFING
1 tablespoon oil
25 g (1 oz) butter
225 g (8 oz) shallots, roughly chopped
225 g (8 oz) mushrooms, sliced
225 g (8 oz) leeks, whites only, sliced in 1 cm (½ in) rings
1 large bunch of fresh sage or 2 teaspoons dried sage
100 g (4 oz) fresh brown breadcrumbs
2 large sprigs of fresh parsley
450 g (1 lb) tin chestnuts, roughly chopped
1 teaspoon green peppercorns, crushed
½ teaspoon salt
1 egg, beaten
120 ml (4 fl oz) hot water

Pre-heat the oven to 200ºC/400ºF/gas 6. Mix together all the vegetables in a bowl with the herbs, oil, salt and pepper. Fill the cavity of the turkey with about a quarter of the mixture then with a quarter of the chipolatas, mixing them into the vegetables. Repeat until the cavity is loosely full, retaining about a quarter of the vegetables. Secure the opening with a metal skewer, leaving space for air to escape.

Heat the oil and butter and fry the shallots gently for 1 minute. Add the mushrooms and leeks and fry until soft but not coloured, adding the sage for about 1 minute to mingle the flavours. Make the breadcrumbs in a food processor, adding the parsley in large pieces so that it is chopped into the breadcrumbs. Add half the shallot mixture and process for a few seconds. Tip the mixture into a bowl with the remaining ingredients and stir with a large spoon to keep the texture chunky as you form a thick, moist stuffing.

Reserve about 4 tablespoons of the stuffing then fill the crop with the remainder, pressing it in well over the breast. Secure the end with a metal skewer. Tie or skewer the legs together, leaving plenty of movement for the hot air to crispen the skin.

Halve the bacon rashers and put a spoonful of stuffing on to each one. Roll into neat bacon rolls and arrange in a small roasting tray. Arrange the potatoes in another roasting tray.

Place a rack in a roasting tray. Lightly oil the turkey and place it breast downwards on the rack. Cook in the pre-heated oven for 45 minutes then baste and season well, spooning off excess fat over the bacon rolls and potatoes. Put the potatoes on a low shelf in the oven. Add the remaining vegetables to the turkey tray and continue cooking for a further 45 minutes, making sure that the top does not overbrown. If it does, cover with a piece of kitchen foil.

Put the bacon rolls into the oven for the last 15 minutes, then remove when crisp, cover with foil and keep warm. Turn down the oven temperature to 120ºC/250ºF/gas ½ and leave the turkey for 30 minutes to rest. Cover the potatoes with foil when well browned. Lift the turkey on to a dish breast-side up and return to the oven for a further 30 minutes.

Meanwhile, make the gravy. Pour off any excess fat from the vegetables and add the cider, boiling for about 5 minutes to mix all the flavours and caramelized juices. Add the stock and simmer for 10 minutes, evaporating down by about one-third. Check the seasoning and strain off the vegetables. Sprinkle in the gravy granules just to thicken the sauce. Keep it warm.

Carve the turkey breast by making a vertical slice each side of the breast bone, then cut in horizontal slices back towards this central bone. Remove the legs and slice off the meat. Take the chipolatas from the cavity; they will have the most delicious flavour. Slice the stuffing from the breast crop.

Serve each plate with breast and leg meat, bacon rolls, a chipolata, stuffing and gravy.

———————————•———————————

ℱARMYARD DUCK

ℳost Welsh farms still have a few ducks waddling around. Some of them become features and live for many years on the pond. The Muscovy duck, with its familiar black and white plumage and red bill, has a reputation for being very tough, but when three to four months old and having eaten a good quota of worms, frogs, tadpoles and pondweed, the flesh is very tender with a good, mild yet slightly raunchy flavour.

They are delicious roast with sage and onion stuffing. When the fat is very crispy it literally melts, and a good sharp Bramley apple sauce cuts through the richness beautifully. For a quicker meal, the breasts can be cooked and served pinky, and the legs made into a *confit* or *salé* (salted).

———————————•———————————

ℬREAST OF DUCK WITH SPICED PLUM SAUCE

𝒜ll supermarkets now sell duck in portions, which is very convenient for one or two people. The best available are generally the Barbary ducks from France. They do tend to have a fair layer of fat which must be cooked off well – white undercooked fat is most unattractive, as is red undercooked meat. But if pink with crispy fat, it is delicious. Taffy at the Hollyland makes a simple yet sumptuous spicy sauce to cut through the richness of the duck.

Serves 2
2 x 225 g (8 oz) breasts of Barbary duck
2 teaspoons clear honey
salt and freshly ground black pepper
150 ml (5 fl oz) red wine
4 red plums, stoned and sliced
¼ teaspoon ground allspice
50 ml (2 fl oz) port
2 teaspoons redcurrant jelly

Pre-heat the oven to 150ºC/300ºF/gas 2. To achieve a good, crispy skin, score the fat of the duck half way through in a criss-cross pattern every 1 cm ($\frac{1}{2}$ in). A small Stanley knife is very useful for this as well as for pork skin or lamb fat. Spread the lean side with honey. Heat a heavy-based pan until just smoking lightly then place the breasts fat-side down and cook for 5-7 minutes until browning well. Do not move or prod the meat during cooking but allow it to tighten naturally. Turn the breasts when the fat is well coloured and crisp and cook for a further 2-3 minutes. Put into a roasting tray, season with salt and pepper and place in the bottom of the oven for 5-10 minutes. If you prefer meat more well done put it in at the top of the oven.

Pour off the fat from the pan, add the wine and cook for 1 minute. Add the plums, allspice, port and redcurrant jelly and simmer for a few minutes to thicken slightly. Check the seasoning and add any juice from the breasts.

Transfer the breasts to a warmed serving plate, cover with the inverted tray and leave for several minutes to set completely. Place skin-side down and carve at an angle to give 5 mm ($\frac{1}{4}$ in) slices. Arrange in a crescent on plates and spoon the sauce into the centre to serve.

CRISPY LEG OF DUCK WITH LENTILS AND TURNIPS

It is mouth-watering to see the wonderful contrast of the pinky breast with the ultra-crisp skin. This recipe has the advantage that it also keeps for ages in the fridge and can be re-heated quickly. Always be sure to cover the meat completely with the fat to seal in the flavours and seal out the bacteria!

Serves 4
4 x 225 g (8 oz) legs of duck
450 g (1 lb) sea salt
4 garlic cloves, lightly crushed
100 g (4 oz) onions, chopped
100 g (4 oz) turnips, diced
100 g (4 oz) carrots, diced
1 celery stick, sliced
12 green peppercorns, crushed
225 g (8 oz) brown or puy lentils
150 ml (5 fl oz) red wine
600 ml (1 pint) stock or water
salt and freshly ground black pepper
2 large sprigs of fresh thyme
1 tablespoon red wine or balsamic vinegar
225 g (8 oz) turnips, unpeeled and cut into 1 cm ($\frac{1}{2}$ in) slices
1 tablespoon oil
2 large sprigs of fresh parsley, roughly chopped

The duck has to be salted for two days to absorb the aromats, so place the legs on a shallow bed of sea salt in a tray. Cover with half the garlic and vegetables, the peppercorns and remaining sea salt. Cover with clingfilm and place in the fridge for two days.

Remove the duck from the salt, rinse well and pat dry. Pre-heat the oven to 200°C/400°F/gas 6.

To cook the lentils, cut several slices of fat from the duck and cut into 1 cm ($\frac{1}{2}$ in) pieces. Fry until quite crisp and some fat has been rendered. Add the remaining garlic and vegetables and fry until just turning golden at the edges, then add the lentils and cook for 5 minutes, stirring well. Add the wine and boil for a few seconds, then pour in the stock, bring to the boil, season lightly with salt and pepper and add the thyme. Simmer for 45-60 minutes until the lentils are just soft and most of the juice has evaporated, leaving just a small covering. Remove the thyme and garlic husks and check the seasoning, then mix in the wine or balsamic vinegar. You can cover the lentils and store in the fridge for several days.

To cook the duck, place in a tray at the top of the pre-heated oven for 30 minutes. Prick all the skin to allow the fat to run out and cook for a further 20-30 minutes. Allow to cool slightly, press into a deep bowl, cover with the fat and cool. Cover and store in the fridge for a month or longer.

To re-heat, scrape off most of the fat (not the skin) and place on a tray with the turnips. Lightly coat them with oil and cook in the pre-heated oven for 15-20 minutes, until the skin is crisp again and the turnips are browning on top and just soft.

To serve, heat the lentils. Place some slices of turnip on warmed plates, cover with lentils and top with duck and lots of parsley.

———————————•———————————

ORGANIC CARROTS

RABBIT

*A*ll around the coastal fringe of Wales, rabbits are plentiful, living relatively undisturbed outside the enclosed agricultural land and along the shoreline. Many naturally venture on to the farmlands where the reception is more hostile. As a food, rabbit is fashionable on many menus in even the top restaurants. Its tender, delicate, yet tasty meat lends itself to an entire range of culinary techniques, from quick sauté dishes to hearty casseroles and curries.

RABBIT CASSEROLE WITH FAGGOTS

*T*his recipe was created when I was living at Rhossili, Gower, where the cliffs are alive with these furry, white-tailed creatures. Also the hearty appetite of the locals required a dish with more bulk, which the faggots give, and certainly a good wholesome flavour. Rabbit can be purchased frozen from most supermarkets, but the livers are usually missing, so use chicken livers for the faggots instead, if necessary.

Serves 4
1.5 kg (3 lb) rabbit with its liver, heart, kidneys and trimmings
1 tablespoon oil
225 g (8 oz) unsmoked streaky bacon, rinded and cut into 2.5 cm (1 in) pieces
350 g (12 oz) roughly chopped mixture of onion, carrot and celery
2 fat garlic cloves, crushed
salt and freshly ground black pepper
300 ml (10 fl oz) dry cider
2 sprigs of fresh thyme
2 sprigs of fresh sage
25 g (1 oz) fresh breadcrumbs
25g (1 oz) shallots, finely chopped
100 g (4 oz) small button mushrooms
150 ml (5 fl oz) fresh or bottled tomato juice
2 teaspoons mustard
fresh herbs to garnish

*P*re-heat the oven to 180ºC/350ºF/gas 4. Set aside the liver, heart, kidneys and trimmings and prepare the rabbit by cutting it first into three pieces – shoulders, back legs and the saddle. Chop the back legs in two using strong scissors and cut up the rib cage along the backbone. Remove the flank and reserve with all other trimmings. Remove the meat from the forelegs and neck. Cut the back legs, the saddle and any other large chunks into 5 cm (2 in) pieces leaving some of the meat on the bones if desired.

Make a stock from the reserved bones and trimmings of vegetables. Boil them together with about 1 litre (1¾ pints) of water for 20-30 minutes, then strain and boil down until reduced to 300 ml (10 fl oz).

Heat the oil in a flameproof casserole and fry half the bacon until just crisp. Reserve. Add the rabbit pieces and fry over a medium heat until lightly browned. Reserve. Add the vegetables and fry for 3-5 minutes, stirring well to colour evenly. Add the garlic, then return the rabbit pieces to the pan, mixing carefully with the vegetables. Season with salt and pepper, cover and cook for 4-5 minutes. Add the cider, heat rapidly to evaporate, then cover the pan, lower the heat and simmer for 5-10 minutes.

Add the reduced stock to the rabbit with one large sprig of both thyme and one of sage. Continue cooking for a further 20-25 minutes until the meat is just easing from the bone.

Make the faggots by roughly chopping the liver, heart, kidneys and trimmings, then pounding it all in a food processor until chunky. Transfer half the mixture to a bowl. Add the breadcrumbs, seasoning, shallots and the remaining sprigs of thyme and sage, and pound for a further few seconds until fairly smooth. Add the remainder of the liver mixture to the bowl and mix well. Form into 8 x 2.5 cm (1 in) balls, put on a lightly oiled tray and cook in the pre-heated oven for 10 minutes until firm. Fry the mushrooms quickly and add with the remaining bacon pieces and faggots to the casserole, then mix the tomato juice and mustard together and add, swirling the pan to combine well. Simmer gently for 10 minutes for the sauce to thicken slightly, checking the seasoning.

Garnish with more fresh herbs and serve each person with several pieces of meat and two faggots.

HARE

The larger relative of the rabbit is a wonderful wanderer of the Welsh moors and hills. It lives a more solitary existence, and its travels and varied diet produce far darker, more flavourful, gamey meat. The clifflands, where covered with gorse and heather, give good cover for its rest time, and frequently abound with hares, which literally squat motionless a few feet from passers by. Years ago, while crabbing at low tide at Langland, I trapped, after a long chase, a fine leveret lost on its wayward voyages around the coast. Later in the day, while my father was eyeing it up for the pot and much to his amazement, I set it free into the bushes.

Hare is highly prized meat in many top restaurants on the Continent. However, in Britain it is often served as an over-rich, highly gamey casserole. The gravy may even be thickened with its blood and cream – a practice that should make it too rich for even the most tweedy country folk. More judicious preparations are, however, most delicious.

HARE BOURGUIGNONNE

Joints of hare are now available in many supermarkets, or from specialist dealers during the winter months. This recipe can be made in advance and re-heated carefully. The flavours develop well after 24 hours. You can substitute beef or lamb meat for the hare, and it is a good dish for older lamb or year old 'hogget'.

Serves 6
3 kg (7 lb) fresh hare, fully trimmed

FOR THE MARINADE
100 g (4 oz) onions or shallots and carrots chopped
2 garlic cloves, crushed
1 celery stick or tops of bunch, chopped
20 juniper berries, crushed
300 ml (10 fl oz) fruity red wine, such as Merlot
1 tablespoon oil
½ orange, quartered and squashed
salt and freshly ground black pepper

2 tablespoons oil
225 g (8 oz) mixture of onion, carrot and celery, roughly chopped
100 g (4 oz) fatty smoked streaky bacon, cut in 2.5 cm (1 in) pieces
50 ml (2 fl oz) brandy
300 ml (10 fl oz) stock
1 tablespoon tomato purée
1 sprig of fresh thyme
4 bay leaves
225 g (8 oz) button onions
150 ml (5 fl oz) sherry
225 g (8 oz) button mushrooms
fresh parsley and other herbs to garnish

Remove the meat from the bones in large pieces, cutting lengthways along the backbone and following the natural muscle shapes. Cut the meat into about 5 cm (2 in) chunks. Chop the bones and make a stock with the trimmings from the onion, carrot and celery used in the marinade. Simmer for about 2 hours, then strain and boil down to about 300 ml (10 fl oz).

Make the marinade by mixing all the prepared ingredients together. Add the chunks of hare, turning well to coat in the marinade, then cover and chill for 24-48 hours, mixing occasionally. Remove the meat, drain well and reserve the marinade.

Heat a little oil in a large flameproof casserole and fry the chopped vegetables for a few minutes. Remove from the pan and reserve. Add the bacon and fry until crispy. Reserve to use later. Fry the chunks of hare in batches in the bacon juice until evenly browned, then reserve with the vegetables.

Return the hare and vegetables to the pan and heat through quickly. Douse with brandy, covering the pan so the flavours will absorb. Add the marinade juices and bits and cook for about 5 minutes, bubbling well. Pour in the stock, tomato purée and herbs, cover and simmer gently for 45-60 minutes until the meat is soft, but not breaking up.

Remove and discard the orange pieces. If you like the dish very rustic, leave as it is. For a more refined dish, remove the meat pieces with a slotted spoon, then liquidize the juice and strain back over the hare to remove the juniper berries and herbs.

In a small pan, fry the button onions in a little oil until just turning golden. Pour off the oil, add the sherry and boil well to form a thick sauce. Quickly fry the mushrooms in the onion oil until just softening. Add the onions, mushrooms and bacon pieces to the casserole, heat through for 5 minutes and serve sprinkled with some freshly chopped herbs.

————————●————————

PHEASANT WITH LEEKS AND SMOKED BACON

The flavour of game birds is rich, almost composty and aromatic. Pheasant, with its magnificent brown-golden plumage and the distinctive long tail of the cock bird, is the most widely available and offers good value, although little of it is truly wild. A pheasant that has survived a season or two in the wild and has gorged on grain in the summer, autumn berries, worms, grubs and roots acquires a deep mellow flavour.
A bird that has been hung for several days in a cool, airy place always acquires a better savour of its wild origin and beautifully accompanies a very rich old Burgundy or Rhône wine.
Reared birds fed on meal, although still tasty, lack the gamey tang of wild birds. Supermarket birds are generally underhung, but will have a good old-fashioned farmyard flavour. You can cook them just like chicken, with a stuffing and all the trimmings. Braised meat makes the best of the body flavours, which render to a rich fine sauce.

Serves 4-6
2 x 1 kg (2 ¼ lb) pheasants
1 tablespoon oil
100 g (4 oz) smoked streaky bacon, rinded and cut into 2.5 cm (1 in) pieces
salt and freshly ground black pepper
225 g (8 oz) shallots, thinly sliced
100 g (4 oz) carrots, thinly sliced
1 celery stick, thinly sliced
300 ml (10 fl oz) rich red wine such as Merlot or Shiraz
2 large sprigs of fresh sage or 1 teaspoon dried sage
150 ml (5 fl oz) stock
450 g (1 lb) small young leeks, quartered lengthways and cut into 8 cm (3 in) pieces
25 g (1 oz) butter (optional)
150 ml (5 fl oz) port (optional)
1 tablespoon redcurrant jelly (optional)
1 teaspoon balsamic vinegar (optional)

Cut the pheasants into four: two leg and two breast quarters. Heat the oil and fry the bacon until crispy, then remove from the pan and fry the pheasant pieces until light golden on both sides. Season with salt and pepper and remove from the pan. Add the vegetables and fry until softening. Place the pheasant pieces on top, douse with wine, cover the pan and simmer gently so that the meat absorbs the flavours. Add the herbs and simmer gently for about 20 minutes, gradually topping up with the stock as necessary. The meat should be almost cooked and will cut easily.

Return the bacon to the pan, cover with the leeks and season lightly. Cover and cook for about 10 minutes until the leeks have softened. Carefully lift out the leeks and arrange on a platter. Top with the pheasant pieces, check the sauce for flavour and seasoning, pour over the pheasant and serve.

To make the sauce richer if desired, add a few knobs of butter, the port, redcurrant jelly and balsamic vinegar to taste.

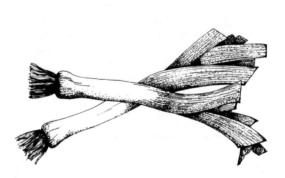

LEEKS

RAGOUT DE GIBIER

This good old-fashioned style of cooking game produces a very rich flavour, ideal for a cold winter day. The lesser cuts such as shoulder of venison, the fore from a hare and legs of pheasant are very inexpensive and tasty, although requiring this longer, slower cooking. Supermarkets now sell mixed packs of game for around the price of casserole beef, making it most economical for a family meal with a difference.

Serves 6-8
2 tablespoons oil
450 g (1 lb) venison, cubed
900 g (2 lb) mixture of game such as pheasant, rabbit, pigeon, wild duck etc, cubed
225 g (8 oz) smoked streaky bacon, cut into 2 cm (¾ in) pieces
salt and freshly ground black pepper
225 g (8 oz) onions, chopped
4 shallots, halved
1 tablespoon plain flour
450 g (1 lb) tinned chopped tomatoes, sieved
225 g (8 oz) button mushrooms, quartered
225 g (8 oz) small carrots, sliced
pinch of dried tarragon
pinch of dried chervil
pinch of dried parsley
450 ml (15 fl oz) red wine
2 teaspoons redcurrant jelly

Heat the oil and fry the venison, game and bacon until browned. Season with salt and pepper then remove from the pan. Add the onions and shallots and cook until golden. Sprinkle with the flour, stir for a minute then return the meat to the pan. Add the tomatoes, mushrooms, carrots, herbs, wine, redcurrant jelly, salt and pepper. Bring to the boil, stirring gently, then lower the heat, cover and simmer gently for 1½-2 hours or until the meat is tender.

SAUTÉED VENISON STEAK WITH ELDERFLOWER SAUCE

*T*he image of venison as strong, dark meat that is tough and dry unless stewed to a pulp is far removed from the succulent, tender, flavourful, lean meat that can be bought from any game dealer or supermarket. In Wales, several venison farms have free-range deer but cull animals when young and tender. All produce first-class, well-butchered and packaged meat which can be treated just as beef, lamb or pork. Many recipes combine rich flavours with the rich meat, but this shows how a light treatment can be delicious, and any appropriate combination of flavours can work with venison just as with other meats.

Serves 4
2 tablespoons olive oil
100 g (4 oz) shallots, finely diced
4 x 175 g (6 oz) venison steaks from the haunch
salt and freshly ground black pepper
1 tablespoon elderflower syrup
120 ml (4 fl oz) Sauvignon white wine
2 tablespoons peeled, seeded and diced tomato or 100 g (4 oz)
mushrooms, thinly sliced and lightly cooked
2 sprigs of fresh parsley or tarragon, chopped

*I*n a large frying pan, heat a little oil and fry the shallots until turning golden. Increase the heat slightly and fry the steaks for 1-2 minutes then turn them and pile the shallots on to the meat. Season with salt and pepper and cook for 1 minute so the meat is still rare. Add the syrup and baste the meat with this for 1 minute. Remove the meat from the pan and keep it warm. Add the wine and bring to the boil, stirring up all the meat juices. Boil for a minute or so to evaporate to about half. Add the tomato or mushrooms, heat through quickly then swirl in the remaining oil and chopped herbs. Check and adjust the seasoning and serve around the venison steaks.

Main Courses - Vegetarian

Root Vegetable Crumble

Gower and South Pembroke have always been known for wonderful root vegetables. Until recently, these gained minimal culinary recognition, and were used mainly in soups, particularly Welsh Cawl, or for school dinners that put kids off swede for life. Suddenly, creamed swede is fashionable in the top restaurants and many Gower farmers are smiling!

This recipe can be adapted for any root vegetable that is available. Small, young, tender ones are considered the best, but always look at the thickness of the skin to determine the age of the vegetable, as often a large swede with a smooth, thin skin, will have grown quickly and will have a delicious, mild flavour. Smaller root vegetables may not require peeling and this will give extra flavour and dimension to this dish. It can be served as a vegan main course or to accompany meat or fish.

Serves 4
100 g (4 oz) young carrots
100 g (4 oz) turnips
100 g (4 oz) swede
100 g (4 oz) parsnip
100 g (4 oz) celery
225 g (8 oz) onions
2 tablespoons oil
1 teaspoon paprika
225 g (8 oz) small potatoes, sliced
4 garlic cloves, crushed
1 teaspoon herbes de Provence
salt and freshly ground black pepper
1 tablespoon mustard
300 ml (10 fl oz) fresh tomato juice
100 g (4 oz) slightly stale brown bread, diced
1 shallot, roughly chopped
2 sprigs of fresh parsley, roughly chopped
2 sprigs of fresh coriander, roughly chopped
50 g (2 oz) butter or margarine, chilled and diced

$\mathcal{P}$eel all the vegetables, cutting into different shapes, and make a vegetable stock from the trimmings by boiling them with water for 20 minutes to make 300 ml (10 fl oz) of stock.

Pre-heat the oven to 200ºC/400ºF/gas 6. Heat the oil in a large pan and fry the onions until just turning golden. Add the carrots and paprika and cook for a few minutes. Add the remaining vegetables, the sliced potatoes, three of the cloves of garlic and the herbs, and stir-fry for a few minutes to colour lightly. Add enough stock just to cover the vegetables. Season with salt and pepper, cover and simmer until just tender.

Mix the mustard with the tomato juice and add it to the vegetables to form a thicker sauce.

For the topping, process the bread in a food processor to form crumbs. Add the remaining garlic, the shallot, parsley and coriander and process with the crumbs, adding the very cold butter or margarine in small pieces to make a herby crumble topping.

Put the vegetables and sufficient juice into a large gratin dish, top generously with the crumb mix and place in the pre-heated oven for 5-10 minutes, until the top is golden and crunchy.

———————————•———————————

HERBS

VEGETABLE AND TOMATO CASSEROLE WITH COUSCOUS

Couscous, durum wheat semolina, is nothing like the semolina pudding that used to be served with a blob of jam in schools. It has a grainy texture that, when revived by soaking, will fluff up into a granular, nutty-flavoured mound that can be used as an alternative to rice to soak up the juices from any casserole, or to court other flavours as a salad or garnish. It can be made very easily and enhanced with other flavours and textures as Dylan Rowlands uses it at his little restaurant, Dylanwad Dda, in Dolgellau.

Serves 4

2 tablespoons olive oil
1 red pepper, sliced
1 yellow pepper, sliced
1 green pepper, sliced
225 g (8 oz) onions, sliced
100 g (4 oz) celery, sliced
2 garlic cloves, crushed
1 small aubergine, thinly sliced
100 g (4 oz) mushrooms, thinly sliced
100 g (4 oz) courgettes, thinly sliced
25 g (1 oz) root ginger, peeled and finely chopped
salt and freshly ground black pepper
2 tablespoons tomato purée
450 g (1 lb) tinned plum tomatoes, chopped
1 teaspoon dried mixed herbs
2 teaspoons sugar
2 teaspoons white wine vinegar
300 ml (10 fl oz) vegetable stock

FOR THE COUSCOUS

225 g (8 oz) couscous
300 ml (10 fl oz) boiling water
1 tablespoon olive oil
100 g (4 oz) onions, chopped
1 celery stick, sliced
1 garlic clove, finely diced
50 g (4 oz) pine nuts, toasted
50 g (2 oz) dried apricots, thinly sliced
1 large sprig of fresh parsley, finely chopped

*H*eat the oil and fry the peppers, onions, celery and garlic until beginning to soften. Add the aubergine, mushrooms, courgettes and ginger, and season well. Add the tomato purée, tomatoes, herbs, sugar and wine vinegar. Cover and simmer for 15 minutes, adding stock to moisten as necessary.

Meanwhile, soak the couscous in the boiling water. Heat the oil and fry the remaining ingredients until soft. Add a little stock. Fold into the couscous, forking well together. Either microwave on high for 2 minutes, fluffing up several times, or heat in a covered, non-stick pan for 2-3 minutes, mixing well. Serve with the tomato casserole.

———————•———————

*B*UBBLE AND SQUEAK WITH TOMATO CHUTNEY

*T*his dish, made with left-overs from the Sunday lunch, uses mashed potatoes and cabbage to make vegetable rissoles. But you can add any other vegetables, particularly swede, parsnips, carrots and peas. This is another dish now popular in up-market restaurants, where the clientele like the comfort of reminiscence about a late Sunday supper by an open fire in the winter. Cold meats and pickles are lifted by the tasty hot mixture of all the left-overs fried to crispy crunchiness on the outside and moist and warm inside. Porth Tocyn Hotel, Abersoch, in north Wales, has been a premier hotel for almost half a century. Its homely style of food is epitomized in this dish.

Serves 4-6
50 g (2 oz) butter
225 g (8 oz) onions, cut into 5 mm (¼ in) slices
225 g (8 oz) red cabbage, shredded
225 g (8 oz) white cabbage, shredded
675 g (1½ lb) cooked mashed potatoes
salt and freshly ground black pepper
1 tablespoon vegetable oil
Tomato Chutney (see page 173)

*H*eat half the butter and fry the onions until soft. Add the cabbages and cook until soft. Add the potato, season with salt and pepper and mix together thoroughly. Heat the remaining butter with the oil in a large frying pan. Add the mixture and push it down gently. Fry until a crust forms underneath. Cover the pan with a plate and invert the cake on to the plate, then slide it back into the pan and cook the other side to another crust. Turn out and cut into 6-8 even pieces. Serve with tomato chutney.

———————•———————

CHICK PEA FRITTERS AND TOMATO SAUCE

Soaking and cooking your own chick peas is really very simple and will give you the best flavour in your dishes.

Serves 4-6
225 g (8 oz) onions, coarsely chopped
2 garlic cloves, crushed
2 tablespoons olive oil
450 g (1 lb) chick peas, soaked overnight and cooked for 1 hour
1 egg
2 teaspoons chopped fresh parsley
1-2 chilli peppers
2 freshly ground cumin seeds
3 sprigs of fresh thyme
1 tablespoon lemon juice
2 teaspoons cornflour
salt and freshly ground black pepper
3 tablespoons olive oil for frying

Fry the onions and garlic in a little of the oil until soft. Mix with all the remaining ingredients in a food processor and make into a coarse purée. Shape into fritters 5 cm (2 in) round and 2 cm (^{3}/$_4$ in) thick. Heat the olive oil and fry the fritters until golden on both sides. Serve with spicy tomato sauce.

———————————————●———————————————

GARLIC

STUFFED MARROW

As a tasty variation, you can add minced beef, lamb or chicken to the stuffing mixture, adding it with the fresh herbs and cooking until the meat is done.

Serves 4
1.5 kg (3 lb) marrow or squash
1 tablespoon oil
225 g (8 oz) mixed onion, carrot and celery, chopped
225 g (8 oz) tomatoes, skinned and chopped
225 g (8 oz) onions, sliced
4 garlic cloves, sliced
4 sprigs of fresh parsley, chopped
4 sprigs of fresh basil, chopped
salt and freshly ground black pepper
100 g (4 oz) bread
50 g (2 oz) butter, chilled and diced
1 tablespoon sesame oil

*P*re-heat the oven to 200ºC/400ºF/gas 6. Spilt the marrow lengthways and bake in the pre-heated oven for 20 minutes or until the pulp is just soft. Scoop out the seeds.

Heat a little oil and fry the chopped vegetables until soft. Add the tomatoes and cook for about 10 minutes. In a separate pan, heat the remaining oil and fry the sliced onions and 2 garlic cloves until golden and beginning to crisp. Add to the other vegetables with plenty of freshly chopped herbs and seasoning. Fill the marrow with this mixture.

Place the bread in a food processor and process into crumbs, adding the remaining garlic and herbs. Add the diced butter in small pieces and the sesame oil. Spoon over the marrow and bake in the pre-heated oven for about 15-20 minutes until golden and crunchy on top and moist inside.

———————————●———————————

CHARGRILLED PUMPKIN

*M*uch undervalued, the range of pumpkins and squashes now available in the supermarkets gives you plenty of scope to experiment with this tasty vegetable. It absorbs the flavours of the rich marinade wonderfully and is simplicity itself to cook.

Serves 4
1.5 kg (3 lb) chunk from a very large pumpkin
300 ml (10 fl oz) passata

FOR THE MARINADE
2 shallots, finely chopped
2 garlic cloves, finely chopped
2 tablespoons olive oil
1½ tablespoons red wine vinegar
1 tablespoon Worcestershire sauce
2 large sprigs of fresh coriander, finely chopped
salt and freshly ground black pepper

*C*ut the pumpkin into 2 cm (³⁄₄ in) crescent slices. Combine the marinade ingredients and marinate the slices of pumpkin in this for 2-6 hours.

Drain the pumpkin and reserve the marinade, adding it to the passata. Heat this through for several minutes to make a flavourful sauce.

Grill, chargrill or barbecue the pumpkin for 4-5 minutes on each side. The dark lines from the charring enhance the presentation. Serve with the sauce.

————————•————————

SOYA CASSEROLE WITH GINGER AND GARLIC

TVP sounds more like a yacht varnish than food, but when called textured vegetable protein or soya meat, it related more to boffin food than gastronomy. Yet the amazingly nourishing and flexible soya bean can be made into chunks that really do resemble meat in appearance and texture, particularly when covered with a sauce. I always enjoy watching self-confessed vegetarians leaping from their chairs when they encounter this 'meat' in one of my vegetarian concoctions. Despite my sincere reassurances, many leave a neat line of these meaty chunks of vegetable on the side of their plates! Soya chunks give a texture to vegetarian dishes that so many lack. If treated as meat and not boiled up into soggy lumps, it can absorb some very diverse flavours. Other vegetables such as carrots, celery, turnip, peppers, swede, leeks or mushrooms could all be added to bulk up this style of dish. Or they could be made into a separate dish to go with the casserole.

Serves 4-6
2 tablespoons olive oil
225 g (8 oz) onions, roughly diced
4 garlic cloves, crushed and diced
25 g (1 oz) root ginger, scraped and thinly sliced
1 bunch of fresh coriander
100 g (4 oz) light soya chunks
½ teaspoon ground coriander
salt and freshly ground black pepper
300 ml (10 fl oz) dry cider
150 ml (5 fl oz) fresh tomato juice or passata
300 ml (10 fl oz) vegetable stock
1 tablespoon Dijon mustard diluted with 50 ml (2 fl oz) water

Heat a little oil and fry the onions over a brisk heat until turning golden brown at the edges. Add the garlic and ginger and more oil if necessary. Add the chopped coriander stalks and stir-fry for a few seconds. Add the soya chunks, ground coriander, salt and pepper and cook together, stirring regularly, until the onions are quite soft and golden. Add the cider and cook for 1 minute. Add the tomato juice and enough stock just to cover. Cook for 20-30 minutes until the soya is soft through but still with a palatable, meaty texture. Add the mustard and roughly chopped coriander leaves and heat through for a few minutes before serving.

———————————•———————————

ACCOMPANYING VEGETABLES AND SALADS

LEEKS

The national emblem of Wales, immortalized by Max Boyce and the legends of transporting his giant leek to support the Welsh rugby team, seems to have been placed firmly in the culinary repertoire. Gastronauts now prepare our vegetable in highly sophisticated terrines, chargrilled with Italian antipasta specialities, in sizzling gratins, creamy soups, crispy fried . . . in fact in every trendy preparation possible.

The leek is the mildest and most succulent member of the onion family. It grows partly below and partly above the ground. The lower portion is white, the upper part green (the colours of the Welsh flag). The entire leek is edible but for the tough ends of some leaves. The most tender part is naturally the white, which can be cut into strips lengthways. The green has a coarser texture and should be cut across the grain. The high water content makes it ideal for cooking in a microwave, which I have found so successful for retaining flavour and crunch.

Wash leeks to remove any trapped grit by splitting the trunk lengthways into quarters and dunking in a bowl of water. The earth and grit will literally drop away, and the leek can be cut into the required lengths.

TAGLIATELLE OF VEGETABLES

This dish can be made in advance, left to cool then re-heated in the microwave.

Serves 4
1 tablespoon oil
100 g (4 oz) onions, cut into 1 cm (½ in) half-rings
100 g (4 oz) red onions, cut into 1 cm (½ in) half-rings
100 g (4 oz) carrots, cut into long strips with a potato peeler
100 g (4 oz) turnips, cut into long strips with a potato peeler
225 g (8 oz) leeks, quartered lengthways and cut into 8 cm (3 in) lengths
salt and freshly ground black pepper
1 tablespoon extra virgin olive oil
1 tablespoon chopped fresh basil, coriander or parsley

In a large pan or wok, heat a little oil and fry the onions over a brisk heat for 1 minute. Add the root vegetables and gently stir-fry for a further 2 minutes until softening. Add the leeks and fry for 2 minutes until all the vegetables are just cooked but still quite crisp and full of flavour. Season with salt and pepper, add the remaining oil and the herbs, mix together gently, then serve.

———————●———————

CAULIFLOWER

The south-west corners of Gower and Pembrokeshire both have mild climates because of the influence of the North Atlantic Gulf Stream current. This bathes the shores with warm waters, whereas similar latitudes over the ocean are frozen solid in winter. Even surrounding areas of Wales suffer severe nights, but Rhossili in Gower usually escapes most frost.

Cauliflower, perhaps one of the most prized vegetables, requires a frost-free climate when the curd is developing, and this tiny area can supply thousands of cases of the vegetable to shops nationwide during the winter months.

When properly cooked, cauliflower can be delicious; the flavours are sappy and fresh. But they become dull when stewed, and the crunchy texture also quickly disintegrates as there is virtually no fibre in the curd. Its high water content makes it ideal for quick-cooking in a microwave, or just in a large pan of boiling salted water.

Cauliflower is a great carrier of flavours from a cheesy sauce to a mustardy piccalilli. As it is so simple to cook, a few alternative garnishes can give variety to this great vegetable.

A cauliflower cheese can be presented as a whole dome or in smaller florets in a shallow gratin dish. Whichever is preferred, the standard cheese sauce can be enlivened with a spoonful of Dijon mustard or sun-dried tomato paste, pesto sauce, or a few sprigs of finely chopped fresh herbs such as parsley, coriander, fennel, tarragon, basil or sorrel.

Not every dish requires a cheese sauce. For a lighter topping and to give an extra texture dimension, make some fresh breadcrumbs in a food processor and add some fresh herbs such as parsley, coriander or basil and some very cold butter to form a crumble topping. For extra crunch, almonds, hazelnuts or walnuts can be chopped in the processor with the breadcrumbs. This topping can be crunched in the oven or under a hot grill.

Cauliflower florets can also be delicious in salads. Blanch them in boiling water (or in the microwave) and cover with a little vinaigrette (see pages 169 and 170) of your choice while still warm. Serve either warm or cold.

Cauliflower soup can be delicious, but not when it is made simply by liquidizing cooked curd, as this makes a thin liquid with no texture. I make cauliflower soup with a mixture of vegetables, even some left-over cauliflower cheese, to give some fibre and make a more interesting soup. Soften some chopped onions, carrots, celery and leeks in a little oil, then cover with stock or water and simmer until just tender. Add cooked cauliflower and fresh herbs and liquidize, adding more small florets to the soup to garnish.

A tasty snack can be made by lightly blanching cauliflower florets then draining and drying them. Coat them in a light batter and deep-fry, then serve with flavoured mayonnaise.

SHALLOTS GLAZED IN RED WINE

*T*he shallots can be prepared separately and used as a garnish for beef, lamb or venison.

Serves 4
12 shallots
1 sprig of fresh thyme
25 g (1 oz) butter
2 garlic cloves, crushed
100 ml (3½ fl oz) red wine
2 teaspoons sugar

*P*lace all the ingredients into a pan and simmer gently for about 18 minutes. During this time the liquid will evaporate, leaving a thick and glossy syrup.

SALADS

*W*alk into any supermarket and the vast array of salad gear in the cool counter shows how this more American style of eating has become so popular in recent years. It's a far cry from the few boxes of dull, limp, flat lettuces that used to be offered. The arrival of the iceberg a decade or so ago brought the idea of crunch back into a green salad, and now at least a dozen varieties are regularly on offer.

I can remember over thirty years ago when local gardeners, particularly my father, in their allotments at Mumbles grew a wide selection of lettuces. The tall, crispy cos lettuce was one of the most popular, but endive, salad bowl, Webbs wonder, radicchio and oak leaf were familiar sights, although the first brown-leafed lettuce was viewed with great suspicion.

At home we never had a salad unless it was 'dressed'. Although very simple, the vinegary sauce would contain mustard, herbs, sugar, oil and vinegar. It was infinitely preferable to the plain salads still so frequently served, which were just as we used to give to the rabbits.

Cucumber, spring onions, radishes and tomatoes were the other essential ingredients in our summer salads, but all were picked daily from the garden, frequently still adorned with the morning dew. Tomatoes ripened in the greenhouse on a sunny day had a flavour that cannot be found in any supermarket to this day.

So I had a great childhood introduction to the delights of summer salads that are now available to everybody every day of the year. All the salad gear can be grown around the world and air-freighted to our shops while still remarkably fresh.

Rather than make nebulous mixtures of everything thrown in together, I like to let certain ingredients star in a dish, and to marry these with the flavour of the main accompaniment, whether seafood, meat, game or other vegetables.

Quantities served for salad dishes vary according to individual tastes and appetite. Sometimes I recommend 'other salad leaves' in the recipes but, generally, any type of lettuce can be substituted. Many supermarkets sell bags of mixed salad leaves in various combinations, and these can be very good, offering a range of varieties that should suit a small group of people. But examine the contents before you buy, as sometimes there is a dominance of the cheapest white cabbage leaves, suitably shredded of course. A party of six can easily eat three or four different lettuces, in which case you can buy the whole individual ones.

A salad dressing or vinaigrette can be varied to suit the main ingredient. The basic recipes are listed on pages 169 and 170.

There are many types of salads. Some have cold ingredients, some are hot mixes, others are combinations of hot, warm and cold, known as *salades tiedes;* some are complete dishes, others accompaniments to main dishes.

———————•———————

SIMPLE GREEN SALAD

*T*his is a combination of leaves – lettuces, spinach, watercress and rocket – which should always be tossed with vinaigrette. It can be served as a starter or to accompany a main course of grilled meat or fish. Always ensure the lettuce is well washed, particularly around the base of the leaves, which may contain sandy soil and grit. Dry the leaves gently in a spinner, colander or on a tea towel.

Serves 4
1 Webbs lettuce
1 small Cos lettuce
1 salad bowl lettuce
100 g (4 oz) young spinach leaves
100 g (4 oz) rocket
85 ml (3 fl oz) Vinaigrette Dressing *(see pages 169 and 170)*

It's most annoying when a salad has large, long leaves that get more dressing on one's face and tie than in the mouth. So combine the leaves in a bowl, ripping them into convenient sizes that can be eaten easily with just a fork. Drizzle over half the vinaigrette, then gently toss the leaves with two large spoons or salad servers. Gradually add the remaining sauce until the leaves are well coated and glistening.

Variations
A good variation as a starter is to make the salad as above but add 100 g (4 oz) of curd cheese to the second half of the vinaigrette and mix to a marbled stage. Spoon this over the leaves on individual plates. This will go well with a fish main course. You could use a blue cheese to go with a meat or game dish.

You can also add some fresh herbs to the leaves, but make sure the flavours do not clash with other dishes being served later in the meal. Light flavours of parsley and chervil will go with most things, but strong aromas of tarragon, coriander, basil and fennel have to be used with consideration.

TOMATO SALAD

Although many tomatoes purchased are lacking in flavour, if you combine many different varieties that are now available in supermarkets, the interesting nuances from each make a good dish. Ideally, buy locally grown greenhouse tomatoes that have ripened naturally in the sun. You can use any combination you like; add some yellow tomatoes if they are available.

Some say skin the tomatoes. I never bother, but if you insist, just have a pan of boiling water and dunk them for 20-30 seconds until the skin splits and can be easily taken off. Then cool them in a bowl of cold water. Always remove the core where the stalk was attached. Never worry if you make too much tomato salad as it is great heated up with a traditional breakfast the next day, or can be used in a soup, stew or stockpot, or frozen for later use. You can add other herbs if you like, particularly fresh chives snipped directly into the sauce or on to the finished dish.

Serves 6-8
225 g (8 oz) marmande beef tomatoes
225 g (8 oz) plum tomatoes
225 g (8 oz) ordinary tomatoes
100 g (4 oz) cherry tomatoes
sea salt and freshly ground black pepper
120 ml (4 fl oz) Vinaigrette Dressing (see pages 169 and 170)
25 g (1 oz) fresh basil leaves
2 tablespoons finest extra virgin olive oil

Halve the smaller tomatoes and slice larger ones into convenient sizes no larger than 5 cm (2 in). Arrange them in a shallow bowl and season with salt and pepper. Spoon over half the vinaigrette and leave for 30 minutes. Snip the basil leaves into the remaining dressing and mix in the olive oil. Spoon over the tomatoes and serve as a starter or to accompany hot or cold fish or meat dishes.

CUCUMBER SALAD

This is another salad vegetable that can be boring, but that responds so well to a lift from some acidity, sweetness and herbs.

Serves 4
1 young cucumber about 30 cm (12 in) long
50 ml (2 fl oz) malt vinegar
25 g (1 oz) caster sugar
½ teaspoon salt
freshly ground black pepper
1 sprig of fresh dill or fennel, finely chopped (optional)
150 ml (5 fl oz) thick Greek-style yoghurt

If the cucumber is young, the skin is tender and tasty and can be left on. If it is tougher, either peel it completely or half peel it in strips lengthways. Slice the cucumber into 3 mm (1/8 in) rounds and place in a shallow bowl. Mix the vinegar, sugar, salt, pepper and dill or fennel and pour over the cucumber. Leave to stand for 2-3 hours. Drain off the juice (this can be added to taste in a dressing) and serve with the yoghurt.

———————•———————

MIXED SALAD

Fresh radishes bring an extra mustardy flavour to a salad. If you can get these very young with leaves, eat the lot, as the leaves are similar to rocket, in fact they are from the same family.

Serves 4
1 serving of Simple Green Salad (see page 140)
1 serving of Tomato Salad (see page 141)
1 serving of Cucumber Salad (see above)
2 tablespoons mayonnaise
2 tablespoons Greek-style yoghurt

Arrange the three types of salad together in a large bowl or divide on to individual serving plates.

Mix together the mayonnaise and Greek-style yoghurt and pour over the salad just before serving.

Variation
Try adding some crispy croûtons to give extra crunch.

---•---

SMOKED CHEESE SALAD

Smoked Caerphilly has a wonderful flavour, perfectly complemented by the other recipe ingredients, but you can use any smoked cheese you prefer.

Serves 4-6
1 large bowl of Mixed Salad *(see page 142)*
120 ml (4 fl oz) Vinaigrette Dressing *(see pages 169 and 170)*
1 teaspoon sherry vinegar
1 teaspoon mustard
4 teaspoons virgin olive oil
salt and freshly ground black pepper
4 teaspoons oil
4 slices wholemeal bread, quartered into triangles
225 g (8 oz) smoked Caerphilly cheese, thinly sliced

Make up the salad bowl. Combine the vinaigrette with the sherry vinegar, mustard and olive oil in a screw-top jar and season with salt and pepper. Shake well to mix. Pour half the dressing over the salad and toss well. Heat the oil and fry the bread to make crisp croûtons. Arrange the salad on individual plates and sprinkle with croûtons. Top with the cheese and drizzle the remaining dressing around the edge.

---•---

SMOKED MACKEREL SALAD

*Y*ou can substitute 225 g (8 oz) of thinly sliced cured Carmarthen ham (or Serrano, Bayonne or Parma) for the mackerel, or use cold roast beef or boiled ham. For a vegetarian alternative to this recipe, garnish the salad with cold cooked beans, cauliflower, courgettes or other vegetables which have been well coated in *Vinaigrette Dressing* and left to stand for 30 minutes.

Serves 4-6
1 large bowl of Mixed Salad *(see page 142)*
120 ml (4 fl oz) Vinaigrette Dressing *(see pages 169 and 170)*
1 teaspoon balsamic vinegar
1 teaspoon mustard
4 teaspoons sunflower oil
salt and freshly ground black pepper
2 teaspoons horseradish sauce
4 teaspoons Greek-style yoghurt
350 g (12 oz) smoked mackerel fillets

*M*ake up the salad bowl. Combine the vinaigrette with the balsamic vinegar, mustard, oil, salt and pepper in a screw-top jar and shake well. Pour half the dressing over the salad and toss well. Mix the horseradish with the yoghurt. Cut the smoked mackerel from the skin in strips lengthways, removing any bones. Arrange the salad on individual plates and top with the mackerel. Drizzle the remaining dressing around and serve with horseradish sauce.

———————————●———————————

*H*OT POTATO SALAD

*T*his is a great dish to go with hot or cold meats, particularly boiled ham. It's also good with smoked cod, haddock, whiting – even mackerel and kippers.

Serves 4
50 g (2 oz) smoked streaky bacon, speck or Welsh fat bacon, rinded
and cut into 2.5 cm (1 in) pieces
225 g (8 oz) onions, sliced
1 tablespoon oil
450 g (1 lb) cold boiled new potatoes, cut in 2.5 cm (1 in) pieces
6 juniper berries, crushed (optional)

2 tablespoons Vinaigrette Dressing *(see pages 169 and 170)*
1 teaspoon white wine vinegar
freshly ground black pepper
2 sprigs of fresh parsley, roughly chopped

*F*ry the bacon until the fat is golden. Add the onions and extra oil, cover and cook for 5 minutes until softened but not browned, stirring occasionally. Add the potatoes and juniper berries, if using, and cook over a brisk heat, stirring carefully so as not to break up the potatoes. Add the vinaigrette, wine vinegar and pepper, heating through well. Garnish with the parsley and serve very hot.

QUICK RATATOUILLE

*S*o often this dish is poorly cooked, with overdone courgettes, almost raw spongy aubergines, and other unmentionables thrown in. I first showed this recipe on a programme called *Summer Scene* made during the Garden Festival at Ebbw Vale in 1992, to go with new season's Welsh hillside lamb. But it's also good enough to eat on its own.

Serves 4
225 g (8 oz) aubergines, cut into 1 cm (½ in) half-rings
225 g (8 oz) courgettes, cut into 5 mm (¼ in) rings
1 red pepper, cut into 1 x 2.5 cm (½ x 1 in) slices
1 green pepper, cut into 1 x 2.5 cm (½ x 1 in) slices
225 g (8 oz) shallots or onions, cut into 1 cm (½ in) slices
450 g (1 lb) tomatoes, skinned and quartered
4 garlic cloves, crushed
4 tablespoons olive oil
salt and freshly ground black pepper
1 large sprig of fresh oregano or marjoram, roughly chopped
2 large sprigs of fresh basil, roughly chopped
2 tablespoons Vinaigrette Dressing *(see pages 169 and 170)*
juice of ½ lemon

*P*re-heat the oven to 230°C/450°F/gas 8 and oil a large baking tray. Arrange all the vegetables and tomatoes on the baking tray. Mix the garlic and oil and drizzle over the top. Season with salt and pepper. Cook in the pre-heated oven for 20-30 minutes until they are all just soft and browning lightly on the edges.

Transfer the tomatoes to a large pan with some of the tray juices and heat through, mashing well. Add the onions and mix well. Add the herbs then carefully fold in the peppers, courgettes and, finally, the aubergines. Heat through carefully, stir in the vinaigrette and lemon juice and serve, or leave to cool and serve cold.

———————————————●———————————————

*H*OT CHICKEN LIVER AND BACON SALAD

I first had a warm salad at Le Petit Truc near Beaune in 1980. Since then I have adapted it in many guises. Now almost every menu contains some variation on this theme. The recipe was basically a large bowl of mixed leaves with some hot fried potatoes, croûtons and some lardons of bacon with a warm vinaigrette. It has been altered to use anything from freshly fried ceps to griddled foie gras. You can also use duck's liver for this recipe.

Serves 4
50 g (2 oz) smoked streaky bacon, rinded and cut into 2.5 cm (1 in) pieces
2 tablespoons oil
50 g (2 oz) shallots, finely chopped
225 g (8 oz) chicken livers, drained
1 tablespoon dry sherry
salt and freshly ground black pepper
2 cloves garlic, crushed
100 g (4 oz) cooked new potatoes, cut into 1 cm (½ in) squares
4 slices wholemeal bread, cut into 2.5 cm (1 in) squares
1 large bowl of mixed leaves, particularly endive
50 ml (2 fl oz) Vinaigrette Dressing (see pages 169 and 170)
2 large sprigs of fresh parsley, chopped

*F*ry the bacon in a little oil until quite golden on the edges, then remove from the pan and keep it warm. Add the shallots to the juice with a little more oil if necessary and fry until turning golden. Add the livers and cook for 1 minute on each side. Remove from the pan and cut into 5 mm (¼ in) slices. Return to the pan and add the sherry and season, cooking for a few seconds to evaporate. Keep warm with the bacon.

Meanwhile, heat a little oil and fry the garlic for a few seconds. Add the potatoes and cook quickly to a light brown. Remove from the pan and keep warm. Add the bread and fry to make crispy croûtons. Toss the salad leaves with half the vinaigrette and arrange on individual plates. Garnish with the croûtons, potatoes, livers and bacon. Quickly warm through the remaining dressing and pour over salads. Drench with parsley and serve at once.

———————•———————

PINK VENISON STEAK SALAD

*N*ot only can you buy venison from specialist butchers these days, but trimmed steaks are also available in most good supermarkets. Cook the venison so that it retains all its natural juices and remains moist and succulent.

Serves 4
1 tablespoon oil
225 g (8 oz) venison steak from the haunch
salt and freshly ground black pepper
1 tablespoon port
100 g (4 oz) smoked back bacon, rinded and cut across
into 1 cm (½ in strips)
100 g (4 oz) carrots, cut into batons
50 g (2 oz) celery, cut into batons
50 g (2 oz) shallots, roughly chopped
1 large bowl of mixed salad leaves, particularly spinach
80 ml (3 fl oz) red wine **Vinaigrette Dressing** *(see pages 169 and 170)*
1 garlic clove, crushed
1 teaspoon mustard
1 teaspoon sesame oil
1 large sprig of fresh coriander or parsley, finely chopped

*H*eat a frying pan or skillet until just smoking, add a little oil and fry the venison for 1 minute on each side, seasoning well when turned. Add the port and evaporate over a brisk heat, then remove from the pan and keep the meat and juices warm. Add a little more oil to the pan and fry the bacon until the fat is slightly crisp. Remove from the pan and keep warm with the venison. Add the vegetables and shallots and fry until golden on the edges but still crisp. Season well.

Meanwhile, toss the salad leaves with half the vinaigrette and arrange on individual plates. Top with the vegetables. Slice the venison into thin strips and arrange on the top with the bacon. Quickly add the garlic, sesame oil and mustard to the remaining vinaigrette, shaking well. Heat until just warm and pour over the salads, topping with coriander. Serve immediately.

———————•———————

GOWER PEPPER AND GARLIC SALAD

$\mathcal{F}$airyhill in Gower receives daily supplies of fresh vegetables from a small market garden a few miles away. The produce includes peppers of all descriptions, garlic, aubergines, courgettes and squashes, charentais melons, tomatoes, every conceivable herb and salad leaves, including rocket. This gives a continental touch to local produce, and a Mediterranean aroma to the locals.

Serves 4
2 tablespoons olive oil
1 red pepper, thickly sliced
1 green pepper, thickly sliced
1 yellow pepper, thickly sliced
8 garlic cloves, unpeeled
salt and freshly ground black pepper
1 large bunch of mixed fresh herbs
1 large bowl of mixed salad leaves, particularly rocket
50 ml (2 fl oz) white wine Vinaigrette Dressing *(see pages 169 amd 170)*
8 slices ciabatta or French baguette

$\mathcal{H}$eat some of the oil in a large pan and fry the peppers, skin-side down and surrounded by the garlic, for 2-3 minutes until the skin is beginning to brown. Season well with salt and pepper and drizzle with a little more oil. Cover with fresh herbs and cook on a low heat for 10 minutes or so until the peppers have softened but are not overcharred.

Meanwhile, toss the salad leaves in half the vinaigrette and arrange on individual plates. Heat the slices of ciabatta or baguette in a little oil in a frying pan. Remove the whole garlic cloves from the pepper pan and squash one each, skin and all, on to the slices of bread.

Arrange the peppers and garlic over the salad with the ciabatta on the side. Quickly heat through the remaining vinaigrette with the cooking juices, pour over the salad and serve.

———————————●———————————

*H*ot salmon salad

*S*almon steaks are so simple to prepare that they are suitable to cook for an after-work supper, yet so tasty that they would pass muster even as a dinner party dish.

Serves 4
1 tablespoon olive oil
4 x 225 g (8 oz) salmon fillet steaks
50 g (2 oz) shallots, thinly sliced
salt
pinch of cayenne
1 large bowl of salad leaves, particularly watercress
85 ml (3 fl oz) white wine Vinaigrette Dressing *(see pages 169 and 170)*
1 tablespoon extra virgin olive oil
juice of ½ lemon
2 teaspoons baby capers or chopped capers
2 large sprigs of fresh parsley or basil, finely chopped

*H*eat a frying pan or skillet until just smoking. Add a little oil and fry the salmon steaks for 1 minute, adding the shallots around the fish. Turn and season with salt and cayenne. Cook for a further 1 minute until just firm, then remove from the pan and keep warm with the shallots poured over the top.

Toss the salad in half the vinaigrette and arrange on individual plates with the salmon on top. Quickly heat through the remaining vinaigrette with the oil, lemon juice and capers, pour over the fish and drench with the fresh herbs.

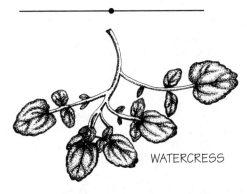

WATERCRESS

DESSERTS

SUMMER FRUIT GRATIN

*H*ot fruit gratins give a new variation to fresh fruits. The warm sabayon sauce under the golden topping sets off the fruit flavours, provided the fruit is ripe and has natural flavour from the sunshine in which it should ripen. Any combination of fruits can be used, but aim to have those of even size and texture.

Serves 4
225 g (8 oz) raspberries
225 g (8 oz) strawberries
100 g (4 oz) blueberries
100 g (4 oz) blackcurrants or redcurrants
1 orange, segmented

FOR THE SABAYON SAUCE
3 egg yolks
50 g (2 oz) caster sugar
120 ml (4 fl oz) fruity white wine

*P*re-heat the grill until very hot. Arrange the fruit into dishes, slicing any large strawberries. Whisk the egg yolks and sugar together until very light and white with a thick and flowing, smooth consistency. This is best done with a hand balloon whisk to gain maximum airiness but it does take some time. Add the white wine and continue to mix well. Stand the bowl over a pan of hot water and whisk for 10-20 minutes until the sauce is very fluffy and becoming warm.

Using a large spoon, completely cover the fruit with a layer of fluffy sabayon sauce, then put under the grill and watch carefully until the tops are golden brown. Take care, as it can burn very easily. Serve immediately.

Variations
This dish can be varied by flavouring the sabayon sauce with some of the following: the zest of 1/2 an orange or lemon, grated directly into the mixture; 50 ml (2 fl oz) of brandy or fruit eau-de-vie; 50 ml (2 fl oz) of syrup of elderflower, blackberry (mure) or blackcurrant (cassis).

The fruit can be set on some fresh fruit 'coulis' or purée – try the sauce from the *Snowdon Pudding with Strawberry and Gin Sauce* (see page 152).

150

A small ball of fruit sorbet can be put in the centre of the fruit then covered with sabayon before putting the dish under the grill. It will remain frozen as the top layer will insulate the sorbet, giving a contrast of temperature within the dish.

The gratin top can be decorated with chopped nuts such as pistachios, which set off a different colour and flavour, or herbs such as mint or lemon balm.

SUMMER FRUITS

SNOWDON PUDDING WITH STRAWBERRY AND GIN SAUCE

*T*hese hot, sweet puddings are reminiscent of school lunches, which were designed to fill the stomach rather than nourish the taste buds. The revival in 'comfort cuisine' has led to many old recipes being revamped to fulfil both sides of the gastronomic equation. Porth Tocyn Hotel in Abersoch on the Lleyn peninsula has been in the *Good Food Guide* for 42 years, and has served these dishes over the years with remarkable consistency.

Serves 6
100 g (4 oz) raisins
50 g (2 oz) glacé cherries, halved
100 g (4 oz) suet
100 g (4 oz) breadcrumbs
100 g (4 oz) caster sugar
25 g (1 oz) ground rice
grated rind of 1 lemon
pinch of salt
pinch of cinnamon
3 eggs
85 ml (3 fl oz) milk
2 tablespoons apricot jam

FOR THE SAUCE
225 g (8 oz) ripe strawberries
175 g (6 oz) sugar
250 ml (8 fl oz) water
50 ml (2 fl oz) gin

*B*utter a 1.5 litre (2^1/$_2$ pint) pudding basin and decorate the sides and base with some raisins and cherries. Mix all the dry ingredients together in a bowl. Whisk the eggs, milk and jam, and add to the dry mixture, beating well, then pour into the prepared basin. Cover this with greaseproof paper or foil and steam in a large covered pan for 2-2^1/$_2$ hours, topping up with boiling water as necessary.

Meanwhile, make the sauce. Boil all the sauce ingredients, except the gin, for 10 minutes. Press through a fine sieve to remove the seeds. Return to pan, re-heat and add the gin.

Turn out the pudding on to a large warmed plate and serve with hot sauce.

STEAMED LEMON AND TREACLE PUDDING

Tate's Brasserie in Fishguard make a simple sweet steamed pudding with a good lemony zing. The sauce can be made for grown-ups by adding 50 ml (a double measure) of gin or Bacardi just before serving!

Serves 4
100 g (4 oz) butter
2½ lemons
100 g (4 oz) caster sugar
2 eggs
125 g (5 oz) self-raising flour
1 teaspoon baking powder
2 tablespoons golden syrup

FOR THE SAUCE
100 g (4 oz) lemon curd sauce
150 ml (5 fl oz) whipping cream
juice and zest of ½ lemon

Line a 1.5 litre (2½ pint) pudding basin with a little of the butter and four thin slices from one of the lemons, retaining the remainder of it for the sauce. Squeeze the juice and grate the zest from the other two lemons into a bowl and mix together with the remaining butter, the sugar, eggs, flour, and the baking powder (this can be done in a food processor).

Pour the syrup into the prepared basin and top with the lemon mixture. Cover with greaseproof paper or foil and steam in a large covered pan for 1½ hours, topping up with boiling water as necessary.

Meanwhile, mix the lemon curd with the cream and the juice and zest of the retained lemon and warm through, whisking for a minute until a smooth sauce has formed. Turn out the steamed pudding on to a warmed serving plate and serve with the sauce.

———————————•———————————

MEDIEVAL BREAD AND BUTTER PUDDING

Tate's also make a fine traditional bread pudding from a fifteenth century recipe. This can be made as individual puddings or in a large family size. An interesting variation is to chill overnight, then sprinkle lightly with a layer of 2-3 mm ($^1/_{10}$ in) of caster sugar and brown under a hot grill; allow to cool and serve as a bruléed pudding. (The fashionable way to brown the top of any bruléed dish is to burn with a blow torch, formerly only used by plumbers and paint strippers!)

Serves 4-5
20 thin slices bread, lightly toasted
100 g (4 oz) unsalted butter
300 ml (10 fl oz) medium white wine
600 ml (1 pint) milk
100 g (4 oz) flaked almonds
a few strands of saffron
4 eggs
50 g (2 oz) sugar
$^1/_2$ teaspoon almond essence
$^1/_2$ teaspoon ground ginger
$^1/_2$ teaspoon ground cinnamon
$^1/_2$ teaspoon ground mace
$^1/_2$ teaspoon ground cloves

Pre-heat the oven to 180ºC/350ºF/gas 4. Cut the toasted bread to fit individual dishes or one large dish. Butter the toast and put four layers into each dish. Sprinkle with about half the wine to moisten.

Meanwhile, boil the milk with the almonds and saffron and simmer for 3 minutes. Whisk the eggs and sugar until frothy, add the remaining wine and the almond milk and essence, combining thoroughly. Pour over the bread in the dishes, but do not overfill. Mix together the spices and sprinkle half over the pudding.

Place the dishes in a roasting tray and fill the tray with hot water to come half way up the sides of the dishes. Bake in the pre-heated oven for about 45 minutes until the custard has set. Sprinkle remaining spices over the pudding.

This can be served hot 'an serve thanne forth for a pottage Gode', or cold.

QUEEN'S BREAD AND BUTTER PUDDING

A variation on the B and B pudding is served at the Queen's Head, Glanwydden. The flavour can be 'warmed up' by soaking the sultanas with 50 ml (a double measure) of dark rum or brandy for 30 minutes, then tipping all the liquid into the dish before covering with bread, which will soak up the goodness.

Serves 4-6
50 g (2 oz) sultanas
½ granary loaf, sliced
75 g (3 oz) butter, melted
6 eggs
150 g (6 oz) caster sugar
900 ml (1½ pints) milk
1 teaspoon vanilla essence
½ teaspoon freshly grated nutmeg

*P*re-heat the oven to 160°C/325°F/gas 3. Put the sultanas into an ovenproof dish, cover with slices of bread and pour over the melted butter. In a mixing bowl, whisk together the sugar and eggs until frothy, then add the milk and vanilla essence. Pour over the bread and top with nutmeg.

Put the dish into a roasting tray and fill with hot water to come half way up the sides of the dish. Bake in the pre-heated oven for about 1½ hours until set. Serve hot or cold.

———————●———————

ORANGE AND WALNUT CHEESECAKE

I like cheesecakes that are almost savoury with astringent flavours and that crunch with fruit zest. The base recipe can then be adapted for other combinations of fruit.

Serves 4-6
225 g (8 oz) wholemeal biscuits
75 g (3 oz) butter, softened
300 ml (10 fl oz) cream
225 g (8 oz) low-fat curd cheese
juice and grated zest of 1 orange
25 g (1 oz) demerara sugar
50 ml (2 fl oz) Grand Marnier
100 g (4 oz) walnuts, chopped

TO SERVE
1 orange, cut into segments
6 walnut halves

*P*lace the biscuits in a paper bag and crush with a rolling pin. Pour them into a bowl and mix in the softened butter to form a crumbly mixture. Press into the base and sides of a 25 cm (10 in) flan tin and chill for 30 minutes.

Whisk the cream until just firm then, using a large spoon, mix in the curd cheese to form a stiff mixture. Add the orange zest and juice, the Grand Marnier, sugar and the chopped walnuts, folding in all the ingredients with a large spoon. Fill the flan tin and chill for 2-3 hours.

Immediately before serving, garnish with the orange segments and walnut halves.

Variations
The citrus fruit can be varied, using lemon, lime or grapefruit. Other types of nuts can be substituted, either plain or toasted.

Fruit cheesecakes of varying flavours can be made by adding 150 ml (5 fl oz) of thick fruit purée. This can be made by boiling 225 g (8 oz) of fruit berries with 50 g (2 oz) of sugar for 10 minutes (with a touch of water if necessary), then pressing through a sieve to separate the pips and seeds. Store in a very cool place.

You can then make the cheesecake with a smooth appearance or leave it marbled with variations in colour. A measure of appropriate liqueur gives extra bite to the flavour. The fruit eaux-de-vie from Alsace are particularly good. Try blackcurrant with cassis or quetch, damsons with mirabelle or gin, raspberries with framboise, strawberries with vodka, redcurrants with Gewürztraminer, blackberry with mure.

CHERRY CHEESECAKE

Another favourite at the Queen's is their cherry cheesecake. This is a very sweet and rich version!

Serves 6
225 g (8 oz) cherries, pitted
100 g (4 oz) sugar

FOR THE BASE
225 g (8 oz) wholemeal biscuits
50 g (2 oz) butter, melted
1 tablespoon caster sugar
1 tablespoon golden syrup

FOR THE FILLING
150 ml (5 fl oz) double cream
100 g (4 oz) full-fat soft cheese
25 g (1 oz) icing sugar, sifted
½ teaspoon vanilla essence

*H*alve the cherries and place them in a bowl. Sprinkle with the sugar, stirring occasionally to form a natural, thick syrup.

Place the biscuits in a paper bag and crush with a rolling pin. Pour into a bowl and stir in the melted butter, sugar and syrup. Press into a 25 cm (10 in) flan tin to form a base and chill for 30 minutes.

Whisk the cream until firm but not lumpy. Mix in the soft cheese, sugar and vanilla essence until smooth. Fill the flan tin with the mixture, smoothing the top, then chill for 2-3 hours. Just before serving, top with the cherries and syrup.

TARTE AUX POIRES

We encountered many tarts on our travels, and the big question was always 'to bake blind, or not to bake blind'. I'm too lazy to go through all that fuss, so this is my advice on tarts! Don't bother to bake blind, cook the tart in one, but pre-heat the oven well, somewhat above the required temperature, and have a thick baking sheet already in the oven, on to which you place the tart to give it a rapid start to the cooking, from the bottom.

Frangipane paste is just a sophisticated bakewell and is very easy to make. It rarely looks right, but always turns out well. Artistic cooks can make wonderful patterns with fruit set in this almondy paste. Barbara Ross at Paysanne in Deganwy, near Conwy, makes this without fuss and it's spot on.
In place of cream, some fruit purée like the sauce in the *Snowdon Pudding* recipe (see page 152) makes a good contrast. You can also vary the fruit to use whatever is available. Peaches, nectarines, plums, cherries, apples, even bananas make a delicious fruit tart in this style.

Serves 6-8
FOR THE PASTRY
225 g (8 oz) plain flour
75 g (3 oz) butter
25 g (1 oz) lard
1 egg yolk
2 teaspoons sugar
1 tablespoon water

FOR THE FILLING
100 g (4 oz) butter
100 g (4 oz) caster sugar
2 eggs
100 g (4 oz) ground almonds
50 ml (2 fl oz) Calvados
3-4 ripe pears
75 g (3 oz) sliced almonds
1 tablespoon apricot jam

Pre-heat the oven to 180°C/350°F/gas 4 and pre-heat a thick baking sheet. Grease a 25 cm (10 in) flan tin.

First make the pastry. Rub together the flour, butter, lard and egg yolk with the sugar and water, to form a dough. Roll out on a lightly floured surface and use to line the flan tin. Prick with a fork.

Cream the butter and sugar together, then beat in the eggs, one at a time, to make a smooth cream. Beat in the almonds and Calvados, then pour into the flan tin.

Peel, halve and core the pears, then cut lengthways into 5 mm ($^1/_8$ in) slices. Arrange in the almond paste, pressing in slightly, and sprinkle the almonds between the pears. Place the flan tin on the pre-heated baking sheet and bake in the pre-heated oven for about 20-25 minutes until the top is golden and slightly risen and the paste has set. Glaze with a little jam and serve hot or cool.

*B*IG BILL'S SCHUMMER PUDDING

*S*ummer pudding from cultivated garden berries has become the dessert for sunny days. Other versions can be made throughout the year using orchard fruits, and even dried fruits, provided the fruit is cooked and sweetened sufficiently. At Hen Dafan, Llanstephan, Bill makes an alcoholic version that's definitely not for the faint-hearted.

This pudding is for autumn days using fruit from Bill's sloe gin concoction from the previous season, as well as blackberries and whatever else is around. His sloe gin uses sloes picked at the end of September with some other berries – rowans, elders, blackberries. These are put into a jar or bottle, covered with sugar, then with the cheapest gin around, and left for nine months at least in a dark place, shaking the bottle occasionally. When the gin is well coloured it is decanted off, and Bill then uses the fruit. All the quantities are approximate.

Serves 6
450 g (1 lb) fruit from sloe gin
225 g (8 oz) sugar
½ teaspoon bicarbonate of soda
150 ml (5 fl oz) red wine
450 g (1 lb) blackberries or other fruit or currants
1 loaf very stale bread, cut in 2 cm (1 in) slices
whipped cream to serve

*H*eat the fruit from the sloe gin with the sugar, bicarbonate of soda and wine, boiling until the pips float to the surface and can be skimmed off. Add the other fruit, bring to the boil, then switch off the heat.

Line a pudding basin with the bread and pile in the fruit, topping with another slice. Press down with a plate or saucer, putting a tin of beans or fruit on top as a weight. Leave to cool then chill for a few hours or overnight. Turn out of the bowl and serve with whipped cream and a glass of the sloe gin. The fruit retains an amazingly alcoholic flavour!

CHOCOLATE PUDDING

*T*his recipe and the two that follow come from Craig Hindley of Portmeirion Hotel. They are in keeping with the flamboyant style of the hotel, where they are served as a trio with a variety of textures, temperatures and colour, although for many one would be sufficient. For this recipe, you need a terrine 10 x 10 x 15 cm (4 x 4 x 6 in).

Serves 6
175 g (6 oz) plain chocolate
90 ml (3 fl oz) milk
25 g (1 oz) butter
50 g (2 oz) caster sugar
2 egg yolks
4 tablespoons strong black expresso coffee
4 leaves gelatine, soaked in water
300 ml (10 fl oz) double cream, lightly whipped
2 x 2.5 cm (1 in) thick sheets chocolate sponge to fit the terrine,
soaked with 2 tablespoons Marsala

*L*ightly oil the terrine and line with a piece of clingfilm.

Gently heat the chocolate with the milk and butter until smooth. Meanwhile, beat the sugar and egg yolks until pale, creamy and frothy, then add the chocolate mixture, stirring continuously. Heat the coffee and dissolve the softened gelatine, then add to the chocolate mixture. Leave to cool, then fold in the cream.

Spoon a third of the chocolate into the terrine, cover with a layer of sponge, then another layer of chocolate, sponge and chocolate to fill the terrine. Cover with clingfilm and chill for 2-3 hours or until needed.

———————————●———————————

CHOCOLATE SORBET

A double Kahlua or Tia Maria liqueur is a good addition to
this sorbet mix!

Serves 6
225 g (8 oz) milk chocolate
600 ml (1 pint) warm water
200 g (7 oz) sugar
½ egg white

*O*n a gentle heat, dissolve the chocolate in the warm water, then remove from
the heat. Stir in the sugar until dissolved. Whisk the egg white until frothy then
mix it into the chocolate, beating well. Either freeze in an ice-cream maker, or
pour on to a tray and place in the freezer, stirring well every 30 minutes until it
is set, then transfer to a covered container and keep frozen until required.

CHOCOLATE SAUCE

*T*his is ideal to serve with a variety of puddings, or even a delicious ice cream.

Serves 6
100 g (4 oz) plain chocolate
25 g (1 oz) caster sugar
2 tablespoons double cream
120 ml (4 fl oz) milk
120 ml (4 fl oz) sugar syrup

*P*ut all the ingredients into a pan and heat through until everything has
melted, stirring constantly. Cook more rapidly for 5 minutes, stirring constantly.

$\mathcal{B}$LACKBERRY AND MINT WATER ICE

$\mathcal{A}$utumnal hedgerows after a fine sunny day exude the fragrance of the fruit of
the bramble bush, which stains the hands to a rich, exotic purple as the berries
are teased from the thorny trusses. The colour also comes through in the
pungent flavour, which is deep and fragrant, reminiscent of its relation the
mulberry, which is a rarity now unless you have a silkworm farm!
Blackberries can be used in all kinds of fruit tarts and pies, and they go so well
with apples in a crumble or pie. As the fruit can deteriorate very quickly, it is
best to cook them immediately. They can then be chilled or frozen. A purée
made by liquidizing and sieving the cooked fruit can be used for cheesecake or
sorbets. The colour and flavour are quite dramatic.

Serves 4
1 kg (2¼ lb) ripe blackberries
225 g (8 oz) unrefined white sugar
300 ml (10 fl oz) dry white wine
2 egg whites, lightly whipped
120 ml (4 fl oz) gin
1 small bunch of fresh mint to decorate

$\mathcal{S}$immer the fruit, sugar and wine for about 10 minutes until soft, checking for
sweetness as the fruit will vary considerably according to the weather. Cool
slightly then liquidize and press through a fine sieve. Mix in the egg white and
gin and freeze in a sorbetier or pour into a shallow tray and put in the freezer
for 2 hours, stirring frequently as it freezes. Serve decorated with plenty of
fresh mint.

SUMMER FRUITS

BREAD AND CAKES

ANN'S BROWN BREAD

At Jemima's in west Wales, Ann Owston makes fresh bread daily, or whenever she decides to open her characterful little restaurant. Their brown bread rolls are chunks cut off baguettes made with a sour dough that is kept from one baking to the next, but you can make it like this without the sour dough, for a simpler recipe.

Makes 4 loaves
25 g (1 oz) fresh yeast
1 teaspoon sugar
450 ml (15 fl oz) warm water
450 g (1 lb) strong white flour
100 g (4 oz) wholemeal flour
25 g (1 oz) rolled oats
25 g (1 oz) rye flakes
25 g (1 oz) sunflower seeds
25 g (1 oz) sesame seeds
1½ teaspoons salt
3 tablespoons sunflower oil
1 egg, beaten
sunflower and sesame seeds for sprinkling

Cream the yeast with the sugar and 150 ml (5 fl oz) of water. Mix together the flours, oats, rye, seeds and salt. Stir in the oil and yeast mixture then add enough water to make a firm dough. Knead until smooth elastic. Place in a bowl and cover with oiled clingfilm. Leave to rise in a warm place until doubled in size. Knock down, then shape into 4 baguettes and arrange on a greased baking sheet. Cover with oiled clingfilm and leave to prove until doubled in size.

Pre-heat the oven to 220°C/425°F/gas 7. Brush the loaves with egg and sprinkle with sunflower and sesame seeds. Bake in the pre-heated oven for 15 minutes, then reduce the oven temperature to 190°C/375°F/gas 5 for a further 20 minutes until the loaves sound hollow when tapped on the base.

BARA BRITH

This traditional Welsh sweet fruit bread is found in every small baker's shop and in the markets throughout Wales. Every baker has a version that varies in sweetness, combination of spices and colour. But the common ingredient is the cold tea in which the dried fruit is soaked for a good tannic flavour! It is also the only bread that is sold in the markets by weight, so never look for the largest loaf for a special Welsh bargain! The bread will keep for two or three weeks in a sealed container in a cool place, or for several weeks well wrapped in the fridge. It is delicious cold or toasted.

Makes 3 x 450 g (1 lb) loaves
450 g (1 lb) mixed fruit
250 ml (8 fl oz) strong Assam or English breakfast tea, cold
350 g (12 oz) stoneground wholemeal flour
350 g (12 oz) strong white flour
2 sachets easy-blend yeast
1½ teaspoons mixed spice
175 g (6 oz) soft brown sugar
100 g (4 oz) butter, melted
2 eggs, beaten
½ teaspoon salt
1 tablespoon honey

Lightly oil 3 x 450 g (1 lb) loaf tins and line the bottoms with some grease-proof paper.

Soak the fruit in the cold tea for 3 hours. Warm a mixing bowl and stir together the flours, yeast, spice and sugar until completely blended. Mix in the butter, eggs and salt, then stir in the fruit and tea mixture, kneading gently for 5 minutes until elastic. Divide evenly between the tins and leave in a warm place for 2 hours.

Pre-heat the oven to 200ºC/400ºF/gas 6 and place the shelf below the centre of the oven. Bake in the pre-heated oven for 15 minutes then lower the oven temperature to 160ºC/375ºF/gas 3 for a further 45-60 minutes until risen and golden on top. Warm the honey and glaze the tops generously. Allow to cool.

BREAD PUDDING

Mr Waldo, a boozer and lecher from Dylan Thomas's *Under Milk Wood*, always had a slice of cold bread pudding under his pillow, together with a bottle of stout. It is reminiscent of tea at Grandma's after the War when every scrap of food was used. It is always rich and filling, the spiciness delicious with a cup of strong tea on a cold winter afternoon, after a brisk country walk. You can use any type of bread, just take off the crusts to feed the birds.

Serves 6
225 g (8 oz) stale bread without crusts
300 ml (10 fl oz) milk
100 g (4 oz) currants
50 g (2 oz) sultanas
50 g (2 oz) chopped mixed peel
50 g (2 oz) dark muscovado or demerara sugar
75 g (3 oz) shredded suet
2 teaspoons mixed spice
roughly grated zest of ½ orange
roughly grated zest of ½ lemon
1 egg
½ teaspoon freshly grated nutmeg
2 teaspoons caster sugar

Pre-heat the oven to 180°C/350°F/gas 4. Lightly oil a shallow 1 litre (1¾ pint) pie dish.

Break the bread into small pieces and soak in the milk for 30 minutes. Stir in the fruit, peel, sugar, suet, spice and orange and lemon rind, then beat in the egg. Pour into the dish and sprinkle with nutmeg. Bake in the pre-heated oven for 1½-2 hours until well golden on top. Sprinkle with caster sugar and leave to cool. Delicious hot or cold, it will store in a cake tin for several weeks.

TIESEN LAP

This is another memory from childhood and Sunday tea with the family. It's a really quick way to make a fruity cake, but it does have a short, rather than heavy, stodgy texture.

Makes 1 x 20 x 30 cm (8 x 10 in) cake
225 g (8 oz) plain flour
pinch of salt
2 teaspoons baking powder
50 g (2 oz) butter
50 g (2 oz) lard
100 g (4 oz) mixed dried fruit
100 g (4 oz) demerara sugar
roughly grated zest and juice of ½ lemon
1 egg
2 tablespoons milk

Pre-heat the oven to 200ºC/400ºF/gas 6. Grease a 20 x 30 cm (8 x 10 in) baking tray.

Mix together the flour, salt and baking powder, then rub in the butter and lard until you have a crumbly texture. You can do this in a food processor if you like, adding the very cold fat in small pieces. By hand, mix in the fruit, sugar, lemon rind and juice, then beat in the egg and milk to form a dough. Tip into the prepared baking tray, piling higher in the centre, and bake in the pre-heated oven for 15-20 minutes until golden brown.

———————————•———————————

FARMHOUSE SCONES

These are very plain and frugal until you pile them high with thick whipped or clotted cream and sweet, sticky, yet delicious home-made strawberry jam. You can vary the type or combination of flours from all plain to mainly wholemeal.

Makes about 10
100 g (4 oz) plain flour
100 g (4 oz) wholemeal flour
1 teaspoon baking powder
50 g (2 oz) sugar
50 g (2 oz) butter
150 ml (5 fl oz) milk

Pre-heat the oven to 230°C/450°F/gas 8. Grease a 30 cm (12 in) square baking tray.

Mix together the dry ingredients then rub in the butter. Mix in the milk to make a soft dough. You can do this in a food processor. Roll out the dough to about 2 cm (³/₄ in) thick and cut into shapes with a very sharp knife to give a clean cut. Bake in the pre-heated oven for about 10-15 minutes until risen and just turning slightly golden.

———————————●———————————

DRESSINGS, RELISHES AND CHUTNEYS

VINAIGRETTE DRESSING

A salad comes alive when dressed with a good vinaigrette. But it's not the vinegar that's important, it's the oil. Even the least expensive vegetable or soya oil makes a good dressing when enhanced with herbs and aromats. Vinegar or acid should be a minimum – the maximum used never more than 20 per cent of the volume. Frequently, the merest touch of a good wine (or sherry, balsamic), herb (eg tarragon, basil), or macerated fruit vinegar or lemon juice is sufficient. The expensive oils, such as extra virgin, walnut and sesame, can be blended with plain vegetable or similar oil.

My choice of oil and acid depends on the main item of the meal. I don't go for a standard film star variety with everything. To accompany poached fish I like a basic combination of olive oil and citrus, enhanced with light herbs, and a more raunchy version with grilled fish. With barbecued, marinated meats a livelier flavour using sesame oil and balsamic vinegar, with garlic and coriander, would be appropriate. There are numerous combinations in between the two.

To make the vinaigrette it is best to put ingredients into a jar with a good lid and shake (like a cocktail bartender) to mix and emulsify into a smooth sauce. It will store for several days in the fridge, and fresh herbs can be added each day.

STANDARD VINAIGRETTE

Makes about 250 ml (9 fl oz)
150 ml (5 fl oz) vegetable or sunflower oil
50 ml (2 fl oz) extra virgin olive oil
25 ml (1 fl oz) white wine vinegar or lemon juice
1 teaspoon Dijon or English mustard
½ teaspoon salt
½ teaspoon freshly ground black pepper
½ teaspoon castor sugar
1 tablespoon finely chopped fresh parsley

Put into a jar with a tight screw-top lid and shake well to emulsify. Always shake before serving.

Variations

For grilled fish add: $^1/_2$ teaspoon crushed green peppercorns and 1 teaspoon chopped fresh coriander.

For shellfish, omit the vinegar or lemon juice and add 1 teaspoon sherry vinegar and 2 teaspoons walnut oil.

VINAIGRETTE FOR LIGHT MEATS

This is a lighter version of a standard vinaigrette.

Makes about 300 ml (10 fl oz)
50 ml (2 fl oz) wine vinegar
100 ml (4 fl oz) extra virgin olive oil
200 ml (7-8 fl oz) vegetable oil
$^1/_2$ teaspoon salt
$^1/_2$ teaspoon freshly ground black pepper
1 teaspoon strong mustard
1 teaspoon finely chopped fresh parsley, basil or coriander

*P*ut all the ingredients into a screw-top jar and shake well.

Variations

For a stronger flavour add: 1 garlic clove, crushed, and 1 shallot, finely chopped.

For cold turkey and chicken add: 1 pickled walnut, chopped and 2 teaspoons walnut oil.

For dark meats such as beef, lamb or game add: 1 tablespoon balsamic vinegar and 2 spring onions, finely chopped, with 1 tablespoon sesame oil.

BEER CHUTNEY

*T*raditional, rich chutneys are wonderful served with cold meats, and especially good to contrast with rich dishes such as *Bubble and Squeak* (see page 131).

Makes about 12 x 450 g (1 lb) jars
2 kg (4½ lb) carrots, cut into 1 cm (½ in) dice
900 g (2 lb) onions, cut into 1 cm (½ in) dice
450 g (1 lb) celery, cut into 1 cm (½ in) dice
2 litres (3½ pints) bitter beer
100 g (4 oz) fresh coriander
50 g (2 oz) salt
1 teaspoon ground black pepper
1 teaspoon ground cloves
1 teaspoon ground allspice
1 teaspoon cayenne
900 g (2 lb) unrefined dark muscovado sugar
900 g (2 lb) currants
600 ml (1 pint) malt vinegar
4 tablespoons tomato purée

TO THICKEN AND FINISH
2 tablespoons mustard powder
2 tablespoons cornflour
2 tablespoons finely grated root ginger

*I*n a large preserving pan, heat the vegetables, just covered in beer, and simmer for 20 minutes. Chop the coriander stalks, reserving the leaves, and add the stalks to the pan with the seasoning, spices, sugar, currants, vinegar and tomato purée, adding more beer as necessary. Simmer for about 1 hour until all the vegetables are soft and the juice is thickening.

Mix the mustard and cornflour to a paste with a little water or beer as necessary and add to thicken, together with the ginger and chopped coriander leaves. Cook for 20 minutes to achieve a good thick but not stodgy consistency. Put into warmed jars, cover and store in a cool, dark place for a week or longer before use. Keep cold after opening.

*L*IGHT MARROW CHUTNEY

*T*his is a delicious chutney to serve with cold meats and cheeses.

Makes about 8 x 450 g (1 lb) jars
1 kg (2¼ lb) raw marrow or pumpkin, cut into 1 cm (½ in) dice
450 g (1 lb) onions, cut into 1 cm (½ in) dice
50 g (2 oz) root ginger, peeled and finely diced
1 litre (1¾ pints) dry farmhouse cider
50 g (2 oz) salt
1 teaspoon freshly grated nutmeg
1 teaspoon ground turmeric
300 ml (10 fl oz) cider or wine vinegar
450 g (1 lb) light brown sugar
225 g (8 oz) peeled and cored cooking apples, cut into 1 cm (½ in) dice
225 g (8 oz) sultanas

TO FINISH
1 tablespoon mustard powder
1 tablespoon cornflour

*P*ut the marrow, onions, ginger, cider, salt and spices into a pan and leave overnight for the flavours to mix. Bring to the boil then simmer for 20 minutes until the onions are softening. Add the rest of the main ingredients, mixing well, then simmer for 40-50 minutes, stirring occasionally and adding more cider if necessary. Finally, mix the mustard and cornflour to a paste with a little water, stir into the pan and heat through for 10 minutes. Spoon into warmed jars, seal and store in a cool, dark place. Keep in the fridge once opened.

———————•———————

*B*EETROOT AND ONION RELISH

*S*erve this traditional relish with cold meats, pâté, or cheese.

Makes about 6 x 450 g (1 lb) jars
1 kg (2¼ lb) small beetroot, washed
450 g (1 lb) coarse salt
1 kg (2¼ lb) onions
1 tablespoon oil
1 teaspoon ground coriander
150 ml (5 fl oz) vinegar
225 g (8 oz) unrefined light brown sugar

$\mathcal{P}$re-heat the oven to 180°C/350°F/gas 4. Put the beetroot into a deep roasting tray, cover with salt and bake in the pre-heated oven for 30-40 minutes until just soft and a knife penetrates easily. Remove and leave to cool. Rub off the skins, which should come off easily under cold water. Cut into 5 mm ($\frac{1}{4}$ in) slices and then into strips.

Meanwhile, slice the onions to 5 mm ($\frac{1}{4}$ in) and fry in oil without colouring until just soft. Add the coriander, stir well. Add the beetroot, vinegar and sugar. Cover and cook for 15-20 minutes until a jammy consistency, adding more liquid if necessary. Leave to cool, then spoon into jars and store in the fridge.

TOMATO CHUTNEY

$\mathcal{T}$his recipe is from Porth Tocyn Hotel in Abersoch. It tastes delicious with *Bubble and Squeak* (see page 131), or try it with cold meats or cheese.

Makes 4-6 x 450 g (1 lb) jars
450 g (1 lb) unripe tomatoes, roughly chopped
100 g (4 oz) cooking apples, peeled, cored and chopped
1 onion, finely chopped
1 garlic clove, crushed
$\frac{1}{4}$ tablespoon salt
50 g (2 oz) sultanas
150 ml (5 fl oz) water
150 ml (5 fl oz) vinegar
$\frac{1}{2}$ red chilli pepper, finely diced
$\frac{1}{2}$ tablespoon pickling spice
15 g ($\frac{1}{2}$ oz) root ginger, peeled and grated
100 g (4 oz) sugar

$\mathcal{P}$ut the tomatoes, apples, onion, garlic, salt and sultanas in a heavy-based pan with the water and half the vinegar. Tie the chilli, pickling spice and ginger in a piece of muslin and place into the pan. Bring to the boil then simmer gently for 1 hour or until the chutney becomes a thick pulp. Dissolve the sugar in the remaining vinegar and stir into the mixture. Simmer for a further $1\frac{1}{2}$ hours, stirring frequently, until the mixture is thick. Remove the muslin, squeeze it out well then discard it. Spoon the hot mixture into warmed jars, seal and store in a cool place.